Haynes

Build your own
Computer

5th Edition

© Haynes Publishing 2012
First published 2003
Reprinted 2004 (twice)
Second edition published 2005
Reprinted 2006
Third edition published 2007
Fourth edition published March 2010
Fifth edition published August 2012

Published by: Haynes Publishing
Sparkford, Yeovil, Somerset BA22 7JJ, UK
Tel: 01963 442030 Fax: 01963 440001
Int. tel: +44 1963 442030 Fax: +44 1963 440001
E-mail: sales@haynes.co.uk
Website: www.haynes.co.uk

British Library Cataloguing in Publication Data:
A catalogue record for this book is available from the British Library

ISBN 978 0 85733 268 4

Printed in the USA by Odcombe Press LP,
1299 Bridgestone Parkway, La Vergne, TN 37086

Throughout this book, trademarked names are used. Rather than put
a trademark symbol after every occurrence of a trademarked name, we
use the names in an editorial fashion only, and to the benefit of the
trademark owner, with no intention of infringement of the trademark.
Where such designations appear in this book, they have been printed
with initial caps.

Whilst we at J. H. Haynes & Co. Ltd strive to ensure the accuracy and
completeness of the information in this book, it is provided entirely at the
risk of the user. Neither the company nor the author can accept liability
for any errors, omissions or damage resulting therefrom. In particular,
users should be aware that component and accessory manufacturers,
and software providers, can change specifications without notice, thus
appropriate professional advice should always be sought.

Haynes

Build your own
Computer

5th Edition

Contents

Introduction

Welcome to the fifth edition of our guide to building your own PC. Technology has changed dramatically since the first, second, third and fourth editions of this book were published: we've gone from Windows XP to Windows Vista, Windows 7 and Windows 8, from dial-up modems to broadband internet connections and from single-core processors to incredibly fast quad-core ones. Best of all, the cost of components has plummeted, so you get more power for your pounds than ever before.

In this manual, we cover two kinds of PC project: a powerful and enormously upgradeable PC that will last you for years and years and a tiny PC that's perfect for putting in your front room – and that delivers an awful lot of power without breaking the bank.

While this book is brand new, you'll find that the important things haven't changed. We keep jargon to a minimum, we explain exactly what components you'll need and where to get them for the best possible price, and of course we provide step-by-step tutorials showing you how to build your PC with the minimum of fuss.

Why do I want to build my own computer?

That's a very good question. After all, few of us build our own houses or our own cars, so why on earth should you build your own computer when you can just buy one from a shop? There are several really good reasons and the most important one is this: If building a car was as easy and as flexible as building a computer, you'd be driving a car that looked like an Aston Martin, handled like a Porsche, had the same luggage space as a Saab Estate, was as quiet as a Lexus and used less petrol than a Toyota Prius.

Building your own computer is the only way to get a perfect PC. So what makes a PC perfect? There are four key criteria. It should fit your needs exactly; it should be flexible; it should be easily expandable; and it should be affordable. Let's look at each of those criteria in more detail.

The perfect PC fits your needs exactly When you buy a ready-made PC, it's likely to be a good all-rounder, and while there's nothing wrong with that it does mean it probably won't be perfect for the things you actually want it to do. While most manufacturers enable you to change various options – so you can specify a slightly bigger hard disk, say, or a slightly better

graphics card – the available options are usually fairly limited. For example, manufacturers typically offer two or three different graphics cards on a particular PC, but there are hundreds of such cards out there. It's entirely possible that the right one for you isn't available from that particular manufacturer – or that if the right one is available, the right hard disk isn't, or it doesn't come with the particular processor you'd prefer, or you don't like the look of the PC's case. And so on.

When you build your own PC you don't have to compromise, so if you want a really quick PC that can happily handle video editing, has all the necessary connectors for your cameras and camcorder and doesn't sound like a jumbo jet when you use it then that's what you build. Alternatively, you might want a cheap and cheerful PC that doesn't take up much room, doesn't cost the earth and doesn't bankrupt you when the electricity bill arrives. Once again, if you want it you can build it.

The perfect PC is flexible The days when PCs were used only for dull work things are long gone, and today's PCs should be able to handle anything you can throw at them – managing your digital photos, editing your home movies, playing games, burning DVDs and so on. More importantly, a perfect PC should be able to handle anything you throw at it in the future too, so for example a PC that's struggling with today's games won't be able to handle the latest releases in a year or two. When you build your own PC you can make sure it's not only powerful enough for what you want to do today, but for what you want to do tomorrow too.

The perfect PC is expandable It's impossible to predict what you might want to do in the future. You might not fancy video editing

now, but in a year's time you might be making home movies of the kids or even making your own spy thrillers in the shed – at which point you discover that your graphics card really isn't up to the job. Or you might decide to digitise your record collection and store all your albums in MP3 format – and within weeks, your hard disk is positively packed. With an expandable PC, both problems are easy to solve. In the first scenario, you'd simply pop in a new graphics card and, in the second, you'd add another hard disk. Easy.

The trick to expandability is planning. If you make sure the PC you build today sticks to established industry standards and avoids technologies that are already heading into history, you'll be able to upgrade it easily and affordably for many years to come.

The perfect PC is affordable When you buy a ready-made PC, it's been built to a particular price – and inevitably that means compromises. You might get a free printer but discover that the machine doesn't really have enough memory; it might include a giant monitor but the manufacturer has cut costs elsewhere and installed a graphics card that isn't really up to the job; it might have the Home Basic version of Windows, which is pretty useless compared to the Home Premium edition, and so on.

When you build your own PC, you decide what your PC includes and how much you're willing to pay for it. Shopping around for components can save you a packet and, if you don't go for the very latest processors, you can end up with a PC that's more than capable of doing anything you want it to do without paying premium prices.

Does that sound like your kind of computer? Then read on.

PART  **Planning the 'perfect' PC**

By doing all the donkey work yourself, you might justly assume that you can build a new computer for less than you'd pay in the shops. The truth may surprise you: you probably can't. But before you return this manual to the bookstore in a fit of pique, consider both the reasons why ... and the reasons why it doesn't matter.

PART **1** Four good reasons to build your own computer

Original equipment manufacturers (OEMs) – or computer manufacturers, as the rest of us call them – get all of their components at bulk prices, so they pay less for their bits than you will. In some cases, that means building your own computer will cost slightly more than buying one off the shelf, but that's not always the case. There are four key reasons why you should consider building your own rather than buying.

UNBEATABLE OFFER

Athlon *XP 5000+++ Processor!*
Massive *256MB DDR SD-RAM*
Super-Big *60GB Hard Disk (5,400rpm)*
Combo *52/ 48/12/6/2/1 x CD-R/RW/DVD+R/+RW*

2 x USB Ports + Modem!   *Integrated Audio!!!!*
15-inch TFT Monitor!!   *Six Speakers!!!!!*
Integrated Graphics!!!   *£££s free software!!!!!!*

CALL NOW 0800 245959

Bargain of the century or a duff deal in disguise? If you've ever browsed the adverts and waded through specs, you'll know just how confusing buying a computer can be. So don't do it. Build one instead.

1. Satisfaction

The second sweetest phrase in the English language is 'I made that' (the sweetest is 'tax rebate'). Building your own computer is an immensely satisfying project. It's fun to do and you end up with a PC that fits your needs exactly.

2. Knowledge

Everybody uses PCs, but how many of them have the faintest idea of how they work? When you build your own, you'll discover how everything fits together, you'll be able to see right through the marketing hype and you'll see where manufacturers cut corners. More importantly, the knowledge you'll gain from building your first PC means that you'll be able to tackle anything from upgrades and repairs to another PC build with complete confidence.

3. Money

Despite what we said above, you really can build a new PC on the cheap. The computing business is rather fashion driven, with hardware firms competing to offer the very latest kit. But the very latest kit comes with prices to match and, six months later, you'll

be able to buy the same components for a fraction of the money. Will you really notice the difference between a 2.7GHz and a 2.8GHz processor? The answer is no – but you will notice a big difference in the price of the processors.

The key is compromise – and knowing where you can cut corners and where you definitely shouldn't. A PC with the fastest possible processor but a slow hard disk and inadequate memory will be massively outgunned by one with a slightly slower chip, the right amount of memory and a fast hard disk. By choosing your components carefully, you can build a PC that will out-perform a shop-bought machine in every area that matters to you.

4. It's the only PC you'll ever need

The projects we show you in this book are designed to be future-proof: by sticking to industry-standard technologies and making sure there's adequate room for expansion, both PCs can be upgraded at any time. Not only do you get to design your PC from the ground up to ensure it does precisely what you want it to do, you can also ensure that you can expand, upgrade and enhance your computer more or less forever.

The ultimate upgrade: replacing an outmoded – or broken – motherboard. But rather that, surely, than shelling out on a whole new system.

Pull the other one!

We know what you're thinking: surely all computers become obsolete in a year or so? We'd argue otherwise. Some bits might not suit your needs in a couple of years, so for example you might decide that the graphics card needs beefing up – but changing that is just a matter of popping open the case and putting a better graphics card in. Faster processor? More memory? A TV tuner card? No problem. Has the hard disk packed up? Pull it out and pop another one in.

The key to a future-proof PC is really the motherboard. If you ensure that the motherboard supports technologies that will be around for a good few years, such as Serial ATA for storage and PCI Express for video cards, you can be confident that you'll be able to exchange components at any time. Similarly, if you look for a board that supports not just the processor you plan to buy but the very latest processors Intel or AMD are making, you can be sure you'll be able to upgrade the processor. And if you stick to industry standards such as ATX and Micro ATX motherboards (more of them later) then one day you'll be able to replace the motherboard and reuse the hard disk, DVD drive, case and power supply. It's almost always cheaper to upgrade a PC than replace it and it's more environmentally friendly too.

When we said that the computer industry was very like the fashion industry, we meant it. Computers are sold in much the same way as designer handbags, with new must-have models emerging every few months. There's nothing wrong with the old handbags and there's nothing wrong with a computer that isn't at the absolute cutting edge either. We're long past the point where computers struggled to keep up with us, and these days a very slightly faster processor isn't going to make your Facebook updates funnier, your internet connection faster or junk emails any less annoying – but computer firms would like you to think so, because their profits depend on it.

Put it this way: would you buy a car and replace it every year, losing thousands in depreciation and sending a perfectly good vehicle to the scrapyard just because there's a new model with slightly different wing mirrors? Of course you wouldn't. So why do it with a PC?

So what's the downside?

Are there any negatives to building your own PC? We don't think so. It takes a bit more research than buying a ready-made PC off the shelf and, if you're looking for the best prices, you might end up getting your components from five or six different suppliers but that's not a huge problem. The big downside is that a retail PC comes with technical support and consumer protection – if you get it home and it doesn't work, or something fails within a few weeks, the manufacturer will fix it. But when you buy components, you're protected under the Sale of Goods Act and manufacturers' warranties, so if they pack up unexpectedly you're still covered.

As for technical support, when you've built your PC, you'll be able to fix any problems yourself – usually in a matter of minutes. That's much less hassle than having to send your machine off and managing without it for days or even weeks while the manufacturer fixes it.

PART  How to shop

There's no particular mystery to PCs: they're all made
with components that you can buy on the open market.
While the specifics differ from machine to machine,
almost all PCs are made of the following bits:

- a case
- a power supply
- a motherboard
- a processor

- memory
- storage
- a sound card
- a video card

All of these things are widely available, and the only thing you
can't get in a typical computer shop is a case that's identical to a
specific manufacturer's one – so if you want to build something
that looks identical to Apple's iMac or a particular Dell, you're out
of luck. However, in the marketplace you'll find all kinds of cases
ranging from traditional desktops to stylish-looking, ultra-slim
designs that look great sitting under your TV. When you build
your PC the problem isn't finding components: quite the reverse.
You'll be spoilt for choice.

OEM versus retail

If you fancy saving money on the components you buy, look
for the acronym OEM. OEM stands for Original Equipment
Manufacturer and you can find OEM versions of almost every
kind of PC component.

OEM versions of products are frill-free; for example, an OEM
hard disk drive will usually come in a plain brown cardboard
box without any bundled software or even cables. Sometimes
you don't even get a box: we've bought OEM optical drives that
turned up in bubble wrap that had been taped shut. When you
consider that OEM versions of products can be 20% cheaper –
sometimes even less – than their retail equivalents, you've got to
really like product packaging to pay more for your components.
Just make sure that you have all the necessary cables; for
example, retail versions of motherboards include SATA cables
for your hard disk and optical drives, so you can happily buy an
OEM hard disk and CD or DVD drive.

One word of warning: if you spot a really good deal on the
OEM version of a processor, it usually comes without a heatsink.
That's fine if you're happy to buy the heatsink separately,
although of course it means a bit more research and a bit more
online shopping. We think the savings involved in buying OEM
processors are negligible unless you're buying very expensive
cutting-edge ones.

New versus second hand

You can buy anything on eBay, and computer parts are no
exception. However, while there are bargains to be had, we'd
advise you to tread carefully. A hard disk that works fine today
might not work fine tomorrow, and of course there's no warranty
on second-hand goods. You'll also find the odd fraudster on
auction sites, not to mention traders who are trying to evade their

Retail products don't just come
in pretty boxes: they include
heatsinks too. OEM versions don't.

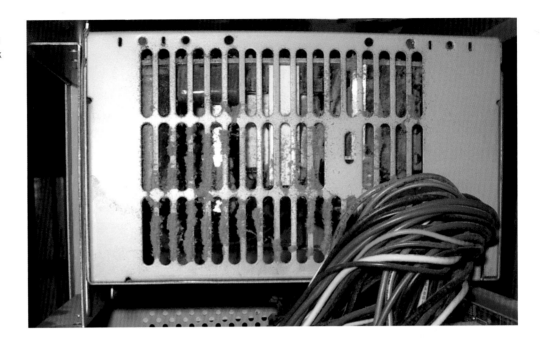

When a power supply unit's air vents looks like this, you can be sure it has been round the block a few times. Nothing a blast of compressed air won't clear, of course, but you have to wonder how much life it has left.

statutory duties by pretending they're not companies. The Sale of Goods Act, which says that goods have to be fit for purpose, applies to retailers but not to individuals.

One reason you might want to consider giving individual eBay sellers a wide berth is the Distance Selling Regulations, which apply to online shops – including eBay shops – but not to auctions. The Office of Fair Trading says that 'Buy it now' auctions on sites such as eBay aren't exempt from the legislation, as such sales aren't really auction sales.

So what advantages do the regulations offer? You can cancel the order at any time before the goods are delivered, or within seven days of receiving the goods, and you're entitled to a full refund including any delivery charges if the goods are faulty. If the goods are okay but you're returning because of a cancellation, you're still entitled to a refund but you need to return the items at your own expense. It's a good idea to pay with a credit card or Visa debit card too, as such cards give you extra protection against fraud and rogue traders.

If you do decide to buy from eBay, be very careful and make sure you follow every step detailed in the buyer protection policies: that way, if something goes wrong you can get your money back. If you don't follow the instructions, though – for example, if you pay by bank transfer instead of by PayPal – buyer protection no longer applies.

Nearly new

Fancy auction-style prices without auction-style risks? So-called 'B-grade' stock from the likes of Dabs.com or Morgancomputers. co.uk can save you money without exposing you to risks. B-grade stock could be customer returns, which can't be re-sold as new even if the component has never been used, or it could be stock that was dead on arrival, returned to the manufacturer and fixed. You won't get much of a warranty (30 days isn't unusual) but you are covered by the Sale of Goods Act.

Whether you're shopping on auction sites or looking through B-grade stock, be careful what you buy: a graphics card in a

grubby box may be a good deal, but a water-damaged monitor or power supply may not be.

The trick to successful shopping is to know what corners to cut. By all means shop around for the cheapest components and don't buy the biggest, most expensive options for the sake of it, but don't limit your future options either: saving £10 on a hard disk isn't a victory if it's so small you'll fill it in a fortnight.

Older but still-functional computers are regularly replaced by individuals and industry alike. Shop around at an online auction site like eBay and you'll certainly find some bargains. Look out for pitfalls, though: an office-based machine may lack a sound card and speakers, and you should check whether the hard disk has been wiped clean of software.

PART ① Where to buy

When you want to buy computer kit, there's no shortage
of firms after your cash. These are the main types.

Superstores like PC World offer a
good selection of DIY components
alongside complete computer
systems. Check the Bargain Zones
for the best deals.

Computer superstores

Superstores are aimed at a fairly narrow group of customers:
people who want to buy a ready-made computer or who need
a replacement or upgrade for an existing machine. With the
exception of special offers, prices tend to be on the high side and
they're usually undercut by online-only vendors – although some
chains are now offering the same prices in their shops as they do
online, which makes things more competitive.

High street independents

Independent computer shops are a mixed bunch in our
experience, so while many small shops are staffed by friendly,
knowledgeable people who happily offer advice, many aren't. A
good independent can be a great ally when it comes to all things
computing, but such independents can be hard to find.

Online

If you don't want or need the personal touch, online retailers
can save you a fortune: they don't need expensive high street
premises and they don't need to employ sales assistants, so they
can sell products at rock-bottom prices. Don't assume that the
site you're looking at is the cheapest, however: prices vary widely
from retailer to retailer, so make sure you shop around – and
make sure you know whether the product you're looking at is a
retail version or an OEM one. It isn't always clear. Watch out for
delivery charges too: some sites charge reasonable postage fees
and some don't.

Dabs.com is one of the largest
online high-tech retailers in the
UK. Its extensive Dabsvalue range
includes unbranded OEM-style
products at rock-bottom prices.

Computer fairs

Computer fairs are regular events all over the country. Here you'll find some of the UK's lowest prices, provided you're willing to haggle a little. Typically you'll find a selection of OEM products, end-of-line products and individual components scavenged from older PCs, making such fairs a great place to find almost anything for building or repairing a computer.

If it's your first visit to a computer fair, we'd suggest leaving your wallet at home. Note the names of traders you're interested in, get a feel for the prices and then go home and see if they're competitive. Official, monthly fairs are well policed by the organisers and regular traders do tend to be trustworthy, but like any such event there may be a few less reliable types. If you follow the golden rules, you should be okay:

- Only deal with traders who openly display a landline number – not just a mobile number – and a postal address.
- Establish with the trader what your return rights are and how you would return faulty goods – and do it before handing over any money.
- Keep all packaging and receipts.

No matter what you're looking for or what kind of retailer you prefer, it's important to shop around. Prices for components can vary widely, often for no apparent reason. If you're shopping online, use shop search engines, such as Google's Products (**www.google.co.uk/products**) and Kelkoo (**www.kelkoo.com**), to compare prices and watch out for sneaky tactics, such as sites that automatically select the most expensive delivery option by default. Most importantly of all, pay by credit card to take advantage of fraud protection and consumer protection and make sure you're aware of your consumer rights in the event of any problems. See Appendix 4 for contact information and useful resources.

Snapping up bargains at a computer fair stall. See Appendix 4 for details of websites that list local markets.

PART 1 Hard and soft options

Building your own PC is actually very straightforward: the hard bit's working out what kind of PC you'd like to build. How do you ensure your PC meets your needs not just today, but for years to come?

Everybody's different

PC stands for Personal Computer, and it's the 'personal' bit that matters: the PC that's right for you might not have the same specification as the PC that's just perfect for somebody else. There's no magic formula to designing a PC, just a question: what do you want to do?

Actually, make that two questions: what *do* you want to do? And what *will* you want to do?

The answers to those questions will help you decide on the kind of PC you want to build. Here are a few examples.

If you want to ...	You'll need ...
Play the latest PC games	A powerful graphics card, lots of memory and a very fast processor
Convert your CDs and LPs to digital music at the highest possible quality	An enormous hard disk and a motherboard with good audio features
Edit video	A fast processor, plenty of memory, a good video card and a very big hard disk
Carry out office tasks	A fairly modest PC with good upgrade options in case you need more power later
Watch high-definition (HD) films	An HD-capable graphics card (or motherboard with HD graphics) with appropriate connectors for your TV and a Blu-Ray drive

As you can see, we have five different tasks that require five different specifications. You can easily see where to cut corners if money's tight: for example, if you want to watch high-definition films on Blu-Ray disc, you don't need a stand-alone graphics card if you choose a motherboard that's HD-capable and you could probably get away with a fairly small hard disk too.

What do you actually need?

In the bad old days, even the most powerful PCs struggled to cope with the demands of software programs. These days, though, PCs can generally handle everything you throw at them. The following table shows the minimum system requirements for some popular programs.

What?	Typical example	Processor speed	Memory	Hard disk	Other
Operating system	Windows 7 Home Premium	1GHz	1GB	16GB	Graphics card compatible with DirectX 9
Office suite	Microsoft Office Home and Student	500MHz	256MB	3GB	
Image editor	Adobe Photoshop Elements	1.6GHz	1GB	4GB	Graphics card compatible with DirectX 9
Video editor	Adobe Premiere Elements	2GHz	2GB	4GB	Graphics card compatible with DirectX 9
Video game	Mass Effect 3	1.8GHz dual core	2GB	15GB	Graphics card compatible with DirectX 9

Looking at the table, it's clear that if you build a PC with a 1.8GHz dual-core processor, 2GB of RAM, a graphics card compatible with DirectX 9 and 15GB of hard disk space, you'll be able to do everything. Won't you?

As you've probably guessed, it's a bit more complicated than that. First of all, the specifications are minimum ones: if your PC meets but doesn't exceed the minimum requirements the programs will certainly run, but they might not run particularly well. Take our video game for example: while it'll run on a 1.8GHz processor in 2GB of RAM, the recommended specification is a 2.4GHz processor and 4GB of RAM. The minimum specifications also mean the minimum amount of features, so a photo editor might work happily in 2GB of RAM but require 4GB if you want to use any of its video features.

The second issue is that each figure is an isolated one, so for example if you're running Microsoft Office and Windows and an anti-virus program and a music player and a chat program ... you get the idea. The whole point of a PC is that it can do multiple things at once, a process called multitasking; if you have so little memory that you have to close one program in order to open another, you're not going to be very happy.

What does that mean in practice? For any PC project, we'd recommend designing your computer around three key components: the processor, the memory and the hard disk. As a bare minimum, we'd recommend:

- a dual-core processor
- 2GB of RAM
- 250GB of hard disk space

That's for very simple tasks, such as web browsing or writing letters. If you want to do more interesting things, you'll need to increase the specification a bit. We'll explore that in detail in the following section.

The more the merrier

If you can get away with a dual-core processor, 2GB of RAM and 250GB of hard disk space, why on earth would you want any more power? Increasing the specification means spending more money. Why bother?

Let's look at our three components in more detail. First up, the memory. 2GB of RAM sounds like a lot, but Windows will take a big chunk of that and various programs will too. For example, as we write this, our email program is running in the background and that's taking up 140MB plus another 60MB for a third-party anti-junk mail package that scans our messages. We're listening to music in iTunes, which is taking another 240MB. Our word processor is currently demanding another 135MB and our web browser's got lots of tabs open, so it's taking 300MB. We're nearly at 2GB already and we're not really doing anything demanding.

It's a similar story with hard disk space. We've digitised our various CDs and our music library is taking up just short of 100GB of space – and we haven't even used the highest possible quality settings, which would make the library at least three times bigger. A

If movie-making appeals, don't skimp on processing power.

few years of digital photos? 105GB. We're already past 200GB of hard disk space and that doesn't include Windows itself and all our various programs. If you're using video, your hard disk will fill up even more quickly: uncompressed high-definition video requires about ten to fifteen megabytes of space *per minute*. The average DVD-quality film is 700MB (0.7GB); high-definition films take up 3GB to 5GB apiece.

Then there's the processor, which is rather like the engine of a car: if you've ever driven a fully loaded car up a steep hill with an inadequate engine you'll know that power matters. With PCs, certain tasks are particularly processor-intensive: video editing, for example, and gaming. While almost any PC is capable of editing a film, converting it to DVD and burning it to disc, that doesn't mean almost any PC can do it quickly, let alone do it while you're getting on with something else in a different program. Similarly, while almost any PC is capable of playing games, not every PC is capable of displaying the graphics smoothly.

Bye-bye beige

What do *The Incredible Hulk*, a tank, a gold Xbox and a collection of bamboo shoots and fake plastic plants have in common? They're all 'mods': standard PCs that have been modified to look more interesting than the beige boxes we've seen for years. We won't be doing anything quite so dramatic with our PCs, but that doesn't mean our PCs have to be dull as ditchwater either. The days when the choice of PC case ranged all the way from beige to a slightly different shade of beige are long gone, and thank goodness for that.

We'll build two very different PCs in the course of this book, one of which will look perfectly at home in a living

Fancy a PC case inspired by stealth bombers? The nice people at Cooler Master are happy to help. They make normal-looking PC cases too.

room setting and one of which will look like a typical gaming PC. If you're wondering why anyone would put a PC in the living room, the answer is that PCs are very handy home entertainment devices: they can use video on demand services, play Blu-Ray discs and DVDs, showcase your digital photos and so on. Our home entertainment PC uses a design that's clearly inspired by other forms of home entertainment technology, but our other PC uses a case that was inspired by stealth bombers.

No matter what case you choose, you'll need to select the components that will go into it. Let's discover how to do that now.

This one's a PC case too: a Thermaltake Level 10 GT Snow Edition case, to be precise. It might look odd, but it's very good at cooling components.

PART  **Choosing your hardware**

Inevitably this section gets a little bit technical but, as always, we focus on what you need to know instead of getting bogged down in jargon and the inner workings of electronics. You don't need to know the history of processors to appreciate that a top-end, multi-core processor is great for heavy-duty applications but completely over the top for browsing the web and replying to emails.

PART 2 Motherboard

The motherboard is the heart of your system and the most important piece of hardware you'll buy. Your processor plugs into it, your hard disk and Blu-Ray drive connect to it, your RAM modules slot into its memory sockets and it might even include your graphics and sound systems. You probably don't pay any attention to motherboards when you buy a PC from a shop but when you build your own PC, it's one of the most important considerations.

A sample motherboard

Here's a motherboard that's very similar to the ones we'll be using in our PC projects: an Intel DP55WB motherboard, which is a MicroATX board. That means it's designed to fit into compact PC cases. We've annotated the key components in the illustration so you can easily see what does what. Every motherboard is slightly different, of course, but the important things are universal.

Power connector

Processor socket

Memory slots

SATA connectors

PCI Express slot

PCI slot

USB ports (x8)

IEEE 1394 port

Ethernet port

Audio connectors

Power connector This connects to your PC's power supply unit. The motherboard then provides power to your other components, including the processor. Really demanding components, such as high-end graphics cards, may require an additional power supply; they may require more power than the motherboard's expansion slots are able to provide.

SATA connectors These are for connecting storage devices such as hard disks and optical disc drives. SATA stands for Serial Advanced Technology Attachment. This board has six SATA connectors capable of speeds of 3Gbps.

Memory slots As you might expect, this is where you install the system memory. This particular motherboard has four slots, although many have two.

Processor socket The processor goes here, with a heatsink on top to stop it from overheating. Modern motherboards use ZIF (Zero Insertion Force) sockets for easy processor installation. This particular processor socket is an Intel LGA1156, which is compatible with Intel's Core i3, i5 and i7 processors as well as some Xeon and Pentium processors.

PCI slot For many years, PCI (Peripheral Component Interconnect) cards were the standard way to expand a PC's capabilities: sound cards, graphics cards and networking cards all used PCI connectors. These days, PCI has largely been succeeded by the newer PCI Express, but motherboards tend to retain at least one standard PCI slot for maximum compatibility.

PCI Express slots This motherboard has three PCI Express slots: one long, blue PCI Express 2.0 x 16 slot for graphics cards and two small black PCI Express 2.0 x 1 connectors.

USB ports This kind of motherboard can have up to fourteen USB (Universal Serial Bus) ports for easy connection of external devices such as hard disks, webcams, keyboards and so on.

Ethernet port Most motherboards include an Ethernet networking port that you can use to connect your PC to a network or a broadband router.

IEEE 1394a port IEEE 1394a, also known as FireWire, is a connection standard for high-speed devices, such as video equipment and high-speed external disks.

Audio connectors This motherboard includes Intel's HD audio technology, a high-quality audio engine that supports full surround sound. Because of this, there's no need to buy a separate sound card. Most modern motherboards include HD audio or an equivalent technology.

There are a few things missing from this motherboard, partly because of space – MicroATX boards are very small – and partly because technology moves on. PS/2-style keyboard and mouse connectors fall into the latter category; most keyboards and mice now use USB plugs. This motherboard doesn't have any integrated graphics, either, and there's no built-in wireless networking adapter – so if you were building a PC around this specific motherboard you'd have to budget for a separate graphics card and possibly a Wi-Fi adapter too.

Motherboard form factors

The technology industry likes its jargon, so instead of saying 'shape' it says 'form factor'. Motherboard firms don't just come up with any old design and hope it fits: they stick to one of several agreed form factors that revolve around the ATX standard. (If you're wondering, ATX is short for 'Advanced Technology eXtended'.)

ATX has been around since the mid-1990s, and it remains the most popular kind of motherboard form factor. However, full ATX boards are quite big and not everybody wants a big PC. As a result, ATX has been joined by three additional ATX standards: MiniATX, MicroATX and FlexATX. Fancy a quick size comparison? These are the maximums for each form factor:

ATX	305mm x 244mm
MiniATX	284mm x 208mm
MicroATX	244mm x 244mm
FlexATX	229mm x 191mm

The big benefit of the ATX standards is peace of mind: you can be sure that if you buy an ATX board, it'll fit in an ATX case; if it's a MiniATX board, it'll fit in a MiniATX case and so on. The standard doesn't just refer to the board and the case: it also

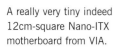

A really very tiny indeed 12cm-square Nano-ITX motherboard from VIA.

applies to the power supply so, for example, an ATX-compatible power supply should have the appropriate connectors for an ATX motherboard. Imagine the chaos if every manufacturer of every component didn't have such standards to work to.

While ATX and its variants are the most popular PC form factors, they aren't the only ones. There's also BTX (Balanced Technology eXtended) and Mini-ITX. BTX arrived in 2004 and was intended as a replacement for ATX, which was struggling with power and heat issues as processor speeds increased. However, Intel managed to address those issues and ATX lived on, leaving BTX somewhat in the wings. Firms are still making BTX motherboards and cases, but ATX ones are much more popular.

Mini-ITX is another ATX alternative; it uses 170mm x 170mm motherboards for ultra-small, ultra-quiet PCs. Mini-ITX boards are designed with low power consumption, effective cooling and quiet operation in mind, although they're also handy for stuffing an entire PC into a non-PC case. As Wikipedia reports, people have used Mini-ITX boards to stick entire PCs inside musical instruments, toys, vintage computers and even a 1960s-era toaster. If even Mini-ITX is too big, then the more recent Nano-ITX standard is smaller still, at just 120mm x 120mm. Such boards are really intended for use in small devices such as set-top TV boxes, in-car PCs and personal video recorders.

You'll be relieved to hear that our projects steer clear of 1960s toasters and hollowed-out toys: we use an ATX board and a MicroATX board.

The chipset

While the processor gets on with the number crunching, the motherboard's job is to get data from point A to point B as quickly as possible – and there's lots of data to move around. There is data to come from and go to the hard disks and optical discs; data to go to the graphics card; data to transfer in and out of memory; data to go to the sound outputs; data to move to and from USB ports and expansion cards ... Imagine an air traffic controller at Heathrow on a bank holiday and you'll get an idea of just how much stuff the motherboard is moving around.

In order to do its job, the motherboard needs its own intelligence – and you'll find that in its chipset. The chipset is a collection of microchips that control the flow of data through various interfaces, known as buses. Each bus has a particular job to do. For example, there's a memory bus for transferring data to and from the PC's memory modules; a SATA bus for the hard disks and optical drives; a PCI Express bus for the graphics adapter, and so on. Recent PC processors have taken on some of this work; for example, Intel's multi-core 'Sandy Bridge' processors handle the graphics and memory, but the motherboard still has plenty of work to get on with.

On the buses

Not all buses are equal. Different buses operate at different speeds. For example, an AGP bus for graphics cards has a clock

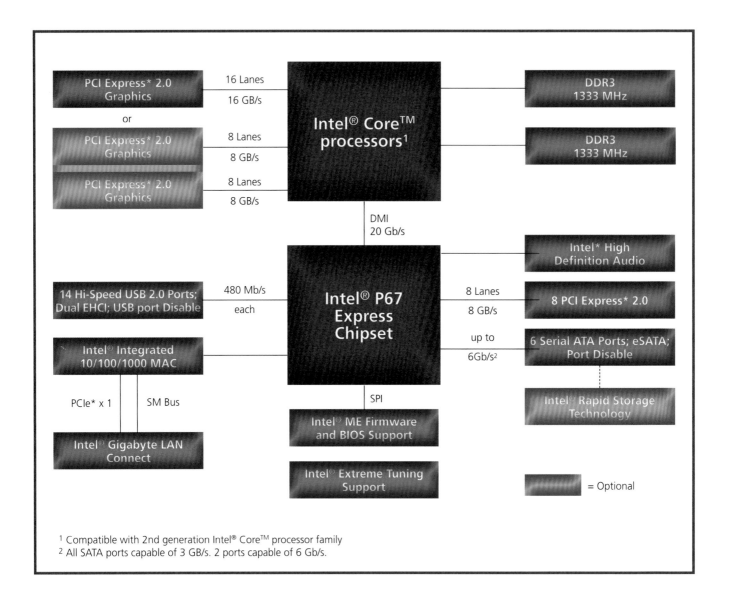

speed expressed in multiples of 66.6MHz, which means that 66 million units of data can be transferred from the chipset to the video card every second.

Speed is only half of the picture. The other half is the width of the bus, which is how much data is transferred in each clock cycle. An AGP 32-bit bus transfers 32 bits of data at a time. That means it's throwing data around at a rate of 266 megabytes per second.

Here's a breakdown of the figures, using round numbers for clarity:

66,600,000 clock cycles x 32 bits equals 2,131,200,000 bits per second
There are 8 bits (b) in a byte (B), so this equals 266,400,000B/s
There are 1000 bytes in a kilobyte (KB), so this equals 266,400KB/s
There are 1000 kilobytes in a megabyte (MB), so this equals 266MB/s

That means the bus is moving enough data to fill a recordable data CD in just three seconds – and in PC terms, that's actually quite slow. AGP's successor, PCI Express, is much, much faster, partly because the interface is faster and partly because it has multiple 'lanes'. Lanes work just like the ones in real-world motorways: the more lanes you have, the more data you can move simultaneously. In the case of PCI Express 2.0, devices such as graphics cards can take advantage of 16 lanes, each one moving 500 megabytes per second. That's a massive eight gigabytes (GB) of data per second. The incoming PCI Express 3.0 standard is twice as fast as that.

Here are some examples of different buses and their capabilities:

	Bus name	Bandwidth
Expansion ports	USB 2.0	60MB/s
	USB 3.0	625MB/s
	PCI	133MB/s
Internal and external storage	SATA I	1.5GB/s
	SATA II	3.0GB/s
	SATA III	6.0GB/s
Graphics	PCI Express 2.0 x16	8GB/s

Chipset architecture

Until very recently, every PC motherboard had three key sections: the northbridge controlled the processor, memory and video buses; the southbridge took care of the PCI, SATA and USB buses; and Super I/O took care of additional ports, such as serial ports. However, recent processor designs have rendered the northbridge redundant: both Intel's Sandy Bridge and AMD's Fusion processor architectures put all of the northbridge functions on the processor instead of on the motherboard.

Even slightly older Intel processors eschew the word 'northbridge': before the Sandy Bridge design came along in 2011, Intel used a 'hub architecture' where the northbridge was renamed the Memory Controller Hub and the southbridge was called the I/O Controller Hub. AMD did something similar, calling the northbridge the System Controller and the southbridge the Peripheral Bus Controller.

Does any of this matter? Not really. What's important is that your motherboard chipset and your processor play nicely together. For example, one of our motherboard choices, the Asus P8Z68-V LX, uses Intel's Z68 chipset. That means it's compatible with dozens of Pentium, Core i3, Core i5 and Core i7 processors. Intel makes its own chipsets and provides extensive lists of their specifications and compatibility on its website but AMD lets third parties make their own chipsets; as a result, researching AMD-compatible motherboards takes a bit more time and effort. The upside is that there's plenty of choice.

Processor, memory and multimedia support

Processor compatibility is the most important part of any motherboard. For example, if you want to build a PC around an Intel Core i5 2500K processor, you'll need a motherboard with an Intel LGA1155 socket. It won't fit in or work in any other kind of processor socket. Similarly, if you want to use an AMD Llano A6-3500 processor, your motherboard must have an AMD FM1 socket. That means it's a very good idea to consider motherboard–processor combinations from the get-go, as those choices will dictate almost every other component you buy.

When you've decided on a processor, you should also investigate the support for other key components: for example, what speed of memory does the motherboard support and how many memory slots does it have? How many SATA connectors, USB ports and PCI Express slots does it have? Does it have integrated audio or video and are such things worthwhile?

Until very recently, the answer to the question 'do you want a motherboard with integrated audio and graphics?' was a resounding 'no', because integrated graphics in particular were desperately underpowered. These days, however, the technology

AMD processors won't fit in Intel motherboards and vice versa.

is much more advanced and integrated audio has effectively killed off stand-alone sound cards (although, as we'll discover later, there are still some applications where a dedicated sound card is desirable). So should you go for integrated graphics too? The short answer is 'maybe', because it really depends on what you want to do. If you'll be pushing your PC to its absolute limits with computer-aided design, high-definition video editing or games, you'll kick yourself if you don't buy a really good, stand-alone graphics card. If on the other hand all you intend to do is watch videos, write letters and surf the internet, integrated graphics will do just fine.

If you are considering integrated graphics, pay attention to the connectors that the motherboard includes: for example, if you plan to connect your PC to a flat-screen TV then an HDMI connector will make things much simpler. We'd also recommend choosing a motherboard that has a PCI Express x16 port so that you can install a full graphics card in the future if you change your mind or if you find that you need more power.

When both video and audio output are embedded on the motherboard, as in this small form factor example, the need for expansion slots is reduced. In fact, you may get away with none at all.

Sizing up the specifications

If you're new to PC building, then the specifications of motherboards appear to be written entirely in gibberish; once you know the language, they're actually quite straightforward. Let's take a look at the two motherboards we'll use in our PC projects.

Motherboard 1: ASUS P8Z68-V LX		
Form factor	ATX	ATX is the standard form factor for PCs.
Processor socket	Intel Socket 1155	Socket 1155 is the socket for many recent Intel Core i3, i5 and i7 processors.
Processor compatibility	Intel Core i7 Intel Core i5 Intel Core i3 Intel Celeron Intel Pentium	The list of supported processors is too big to print here – check http://uk.asus.com/Motherboards/Intel_Socket_1155/P8Z68V_LX for the full list – but, as you can see, if it's recent and made by Intel, this motherboard can handle it. Always check the compatibility lists, though!
Supported RAM	DDR3	DDR3 is the most widely supported and fastest kind of memory available.
Maximum RAM	32GB	32GB is a ridiculously large amount of memory, but it's nice to have room for expansion.
Supported RAM speeds	2200,2133,1866,1600,1333, 1066MHz	You'll need to know these speeds when you shop for memory. Due to a CPU quirk, 2200, 2000, and 1800MHz memory actually run at 2133, 1866 and 1600MHz respectively.
Integrated video	LucidLogix Virtu	This system is quite clever: if you've got a graphics card installed as well, it switches between integrated graphics and the graphics card depending on what's the best option at the time.
Integrated audio	Realtek HD Audio	This is a popular and very good surround sound audio system.
Expansion slots	1 x PCIe 2.0 x 16 1 x PCIe 2.0 x 16 (x4 mode) 2 x PCIe 2.0 x 1 3 x PCI	The PCIe x 16 slots are for high-end graphics cards, while the PCIe 2.0 x 1 slots are for expansion cards. The PCI slots are for installing older PCI cards.
Storage interfaces	2 x SATA 6Gb/s 4 x SATA 3Gb/s	This motherboard supports the very fastest 6Gb/s SATA interface for super-fast hard disks but also has slower SATA ports for devices, such as DVD drives, that don't need the speed.
Other ports	1 x PS/2 1 x DVI 1 x D-Sub 1 x HDMI 1 x LAN 2 x USB 3.0 4 x USB 2.0 1 x Optical S/PDIF 6 x audio jacks	For connecting an older keyboard or mouse. For connecting to the integrated graphics. For connecting to the integrated graphics. For connecting to the integrated graphics. The obligatory Ethernet port for networking. Two super-fast USB 3.0 ports. Four standard USB ports. For connecting high-end hi-fi kit. For connecting surround-sound speakers.

It's a lot less intimidating in plain English, isn't it? We can now see that this particular motherboard supports Core i3, i5 and i7 processors, doesn't need a sound card, supports every major modern kind of connection and will fit in an ATX case. Excellent. Let's look at another one.

Motherboard 2: Asrock A75M-HVS		
Form factor	MicroATX	This motherboard is a little bit smaller than a standard ATX board, so it needs a MicroATX case.
Processor socket	FM1	This is the socket for recent AMD processors.
Processor compatibility	AMD Sempron AMD Athlon AMD A4 AMD E2 AMD A6 AMD A8	The full compatibility list is at www.asrock.com/mb/overview. asp?model=a75m-hvs but, as you can see, most recent AMD processors are fully supported.
Supported RAM	DDR3	Once again, this motherboard supports the most popular and fastest memory technology.
Maximum RAM	16GB	This board only has two memory slots, although there's room for a very respectable 16GB.
Supported RAM speeds	2400, 1866, 1600, 1333, 1066, 800MHz	These are the memory speeds we'll need to look for when we go shopping.
Integrated video	AMD Radeon HD	AMD's Radeon graphics technology is very good and perfectly capable of playing HD video.
Integrated audio	VIA HD Audio	VIA's high-definition audio system is a popular and reliable choice.
Expansion slots	1 x PCIe 2.0 x 16 1 x PCIe 2.0 x 1 1 x PCI	The first PCIe slot is for a high-end graphics card, although you don't really need one for everyday tasks. The other two slots are for expansion cards.
Storage interfaces	6 x SATA III 6.0Gb/s	This board supports the very fastest storage interface, SATA III.
Other ports	2 x PS/2 1 x D-Sub 1 x HDMI 4 x USB 3.0 2 x USB 2.0 1 x LAN 3 x HD audio jacks	For connecting older keyboards and mice. For connecting to the integrated graphics. For connecting to the integrated graphics. Four super-speedy USB ports. Two standard USB ports. The obligatory Ethernet port for networking. Line in, speaker out and microphone jacks.

Once again, it's a lot better in English: we can see that the board requires an AMD processor, supports fast DDR3 memory and has lots of expansion and connection options. It also has quite powerful integrated graphics, so we can manage quite happily without a dedicated graphics card.

It's worth mentioning that when a motherboard lists the available ports – for example, the Asrock board above has two USB ports – that doesn't mean you can't add more. Most motherboards have additional connectors for USB ports, which you can then connect to the USB ports that come on the front of some PC cases. We'll do that with our two PC projects.

Chipset drivers You can't upgrade the chipset on an old motherboard but you can and should upgrade the chipset drivers periodically. Sometimes, motherboards are rushed to market and the software that controls the chipset – and hence the entire computer – doesn't work as it should. Sometimes it's downright broken. A driver update is often sufficient to bring the chipset up to speed and hence make the difference between a useful motherboard and a waste of money. Driver updates can also improve chipset performance in a key area such as integrated video. Pay occasional visits to the motherboard or chipset manufacturer's website and look for downloadable driver updates. We should also point out that the risk of running into driver and performance problems is significantly higher if you buy the very latest motherboard and/or chipset on the market, particularly when it's a motherboard manufacturer's first outing with that particular chipset. Why not let others have the headaches and plump for an almost-but-not-quite-spanking-new chipset where early teething troubles will have come to light and (hopefully) been remedied at source?

Intel, AMD and picking the perfect processor

As you've already spotted, Intel and its arch-rival AMD do things differently – so you can't put an AMD processor in a motherboard designed for Intel chips and vice versa. More importantly, you can't directly compare an Intel processor with an AMD one, because even if they have the same processor speeds the differences in the way they're made means you'd have more luck comparing apples and badgers. For example, when technology site Tom's Hardware compared Intel and AMD's processor ranges, it found that AMD's Phenom X4 9700 – a quad-core processor running at 2.4GHz – delivered almost identical performance to Intel's Core 2 Duo E6550, which is a dual-core processor running at 2.33GHz. However, that doesn't mean the Intel processor is faster: if software isn't designed to take advantage of multi-core processors, they won't be running at full power.

There's also money to consider. AMD processors can be pricier than the equivalent Intel ones, but AMD motherboards tend to be cheaper – and you'll often find (as we did when we built our small form factor PC) that an AMD processor–motherboard combination offers all the features you want at a much lower price than the Intel equivalent.

So which should you choose – Intel or AMD? The short answer is 'whichever you prefer'. While comparisons between Intel and AMD processors are largely meaningless, you can use the speeds to compare different processors from the same range – so you can expect a 2.66GHz processor to run slightly faster than a 2.4GHz one and considerably faster than a 1.8GHz one. We'd recommend setting a budget, seeing what Intel and AMD offer within your price bracket and then checking out a site, such as **www.extremetech.com**, to see how your shortlisted processors perform in real-world tests.

Chipset Conundrums

If you're considering an Intel-based PC, choosing a motherboard is straightforward enough: just find the right Intel chipset and everything follows from that. You'll find full details of Intel's chipset range at **www.intel.com/products/chipsets**. However, if you'd rather build an AMD-based system you'll need to delve a little deeper and find out what motherboards are available for your chosen processor.

That's something you should do anyway, because motherboards are not created equal. Different firms implement chipsets in different ways, so one firm might offer four PCI slots while another's otherwise identical motherboard offers six, or it might offer four USB ports while a rival firm's board gives you eight. There can be other differences too. Some motherboards supplement their audio connectors with digital outputs that you can connect to high-end audio equipment, while others have built-in wireless networking. Even within their own ranges, manufacturers have a seemingly endless list of motherboards based around a standard chipset but with each one offering slightly different connections or designs.

What that all means is that while it's important to choose the right chipset, unfortunately you'll still need to wade through different motherboards' specification sheets to make sure you're getting the one you really want. If you understand what the different specifications mean and have a clear idea of the kind of PC you want to build, picking the right motherboard is easy – and once you've chosen that, everything else falls swiftly into place.

For every Intel processor, there's an AMD alternative. This is the AMD Athlon 64 X2, a direct rival to dual-core Intel chips.

PART **Processor**

The central processing unit – CPU or processor for short – is the engine of every PC and, in recent years, it's become quite incredibly powerful. It's also become a powerful marketing tool, with adverts urging you to buy a PC because it's got a Core i7 in it, or an AMD A8. However, like the engines in cars, it's not always the best idea to buy the biggest, most powerful processor you can find. There's more to processor choice than sheer power.

There are two very good reasons why you shouldn't break the bank by buying the very latest, most powerful CPUs. The first is that they're frighteningly expensive, and the second is that you probably don't need them and won't get any significant benefit from buying them over more affordable options.

Let's say you want a PC that can handle absolutely everything. The Core i7 Extreme Edition 3.3GHz processor certainly fits the bill, but we've just looked on Misco UK's website and it's £844 including delivery. A 3.3GHz Core i5 2500K is a much more reasonable £150, and we can promise you that it's very, very fast. By going for the Core i5, we can build an entire PC for less than the price of that single Core i7 processor.

It's a similar story with AMD processors, although the figures aren't quite so frightening. Where Dabs.com sells the AMD

At the time of writing, the Core i7 is the most powerful desktop PC processor that Intel makes.

If you buy an Intel processor in retail packaging, the box also includes the processor heatsink and cooling fan. If you go for a cheaper OEM version, the heatsink isn't included.

FX-8150 processor with liquid cooling for £269, an AMD A6-3500 running at 2.1GHz is £200 cheaper. It's not as fast, but it's perfectly capable of everyday computing and home entertainment duties.

The truth is, processor speed is only part of the equation: a fast processor in a PC with insufficient memory will be hopeless, and no amount of processor power will make your typing any faster or your Facebook updates any funnier. By all means buy the fastest processor you can afford, but don't do it at the expense of everything else. There's no point in having the fastest CPU around if you then have to cut corners on the memory, on the hard disk and on other crucial components.

Processor evolution

Processors have evolved in three key areas. They've become faster; they've become multi-core; and they've taken on some of the work that the motherboard used to do. The real story is a little bit more complicated than that, however, because it turns out that you can't just make PC processors go faster and faster. Sooner or later, you run up against the laws of physics.

Before Intel moved to the Core processor, the predecessor of today's Core i3, i5 and i7 processors, its flagship desktop processor was the Pentium. The Pentium got faster and faster, and everybody expected it to reach speeds as high as 10GHz, but then something odd happened: at around 3.8GHz, the Pentium hit the buffers. There were several reasons for that. The big one was heat – the faster a processor runs, the more heat it generates and battling that heat is a constant problem for processor designers – but the Pentium suffered from a fairly inefficient design too.

Intel went back to the drawing board and came up with the Core processor range. Instead of one processor driven as hard as possible, processors such as the Core Duo had twin processors integrated into a single CPU. On paper, the clock speeds – the measure of how fast a processor can work, in millions (MHz) or billions (GHz) per second – were lower than the equivalent Pentiums, but the Core processors were much more efficient and delivered much better performance.

Manufacturing moved to ever-smaller sizes and processors became faster and more energy efficient. Dual-core processors became quad-core processors and speeds increased: today, the Core i7-975 Extreme Edition has four processor cores running at 3.33GHz. AMD processors underwent a similar evolution, with the A10-5800K 'Trinity' processor running four cores at up to 4.2GHz.

Whether you choose Intel or AMD for your processor, it's worth remembering that, generally speaking, the more powerful the processor, the more power it will use. The fastest model in a particular processor line-up is likely to draw more power and emit more heat than slower models, and as a result it may require a beefier power supply and a better cooling system.

Two cores, or even more?

Comparing processors used to be simple: a 2GHz processor would run twice as quickly as a 1GHz one. Not any more, and not if you're trying to compare AMD and Intel processors. The difference in architecture between an AMD processor and an Intel one is so great that trying to compare them on clock speeds is completely meaningless: the only way to get a decent comparison is to read head-to-head reviews on sites such as www.extremetech.com.

The key advantage of multi-core processors is that they multitask properly. Single-core processors generally pretended to do more than one thing at a time: they switched between different tasks at high speed, so they appeared to be doing several things at once. With multi-core processors, however, PCs genuinely are doing multiple things at the same time. Provided your software can take advantage of it – and every version of Windows since Windows XP can do – then your computing experience should be faster and smoother on a multi-core system than on a single-core one.

For really demanding jobs (such as editing enormous high-resolution digital photos, editing or converting high-definition video, or rendering 3D graphics), a quad-core processor will massively reduce the amount of time those tasks take – and the faster the quad-core processor, the more time you'll save. The question is whether that time saving is worth the extra expense because, of course, more power means more money. That's one for you to decide!

Celerons and other options

So far we've concentrated on the higher-end processors from Intel (the Core i3, i5 and i7 processors) and AMD (the AMD Fusion). However, they're not the only options. Here are some of the other processors you might encounter online. Remember that some of them will require specialist motherboards; for example, some Intel Celerons need to be paired with motherboards that have LGA775 sockets rather than the more recent LGA1155.

Intel Atom   This low-power processor was designed for energy efficiency rather than sheer speed and it's the processor of choice in cheap and cheerful netbooks. There's a place for the Atom if you're planning to make a very small, quiet, energy-efficient PC but it doesn't really have the horsepower we need in our PC projects.

Intel Celeron   Originally designed for laptops, the Celeron is a kind of Tesco Value processor: it looks and works like Intel's other processors, but it's a lot cheaper and isn't quite as powerful. If you're on a really tight budget, the Celeron is worth considering but don't expect Tesco Finest performance.

Intel Pentium   Yes, it's still going and there are plenty of processors in the sub-£60 price bracket now. It's not a bad processor by any means, but the newer Core processors are better and aren't considerably more expensive.

AMD A4   AMD's entry-level processor is very cheap – a 2.5GHz one costs around £35 online – but it's dual core compared to the three or four cores of its big brother, the A6. It's not as powerful and it's not much cheaper.

AMD Phenom II   Designed for high-performance computing and gaming, AMD's Phenom processors pack a powerful punch. The Phenom II X6, for example, is a six-core, 2.8GHz processor. If you go for one of these, you'll need a motherboard packing an AM3 socket, not the FM1 socket in our AMD-powered project.

AMD's Phenom is a very powerful six-core processor that packs a hefty punch. It's a good choice for gaming systems.

They come in many shapes and sizes but, stylish or otherwise, a heatsink is an essential accoutrement for a hot CPU.

Cooling

Processors get very, very hot when in use and need to be adequately cooled. This usually involves a heatsink unit with a built-in fan that attaches directly to the processor by means of clips. The heatsink has aluminium fins that dissipate heat generated by the hot core of the processor and the fan cools it with a constant flow of air. Many motherboards also have a secondary heatsink to cool the northbridge chip.

Without a heatsink, a processor would soon overheat and either shut itself down, if you are lucky, or burn out completely and probably take the motherboard with it.

All retail processors ship with suitable units in the box. Indeed, this is one very good reason to pay a little more for the retail packaging. If you source an OEM processor – i.e. one originally supplied to a computer manufacturer and later resold – you will also have to buy a compatible heatsink/fan. This is no great problem but do be sure to get one rated for the clock speed of your processor. It must also be designed for the appropriate socket i.e. a Socket 775 heatsink won't fit in a Socket 478 motherboard.

We cover the installation of heatsinks in detail later. See also Appendix 1 on quiet PCs.

PART  **Memory**

System memory – Random Access Memory (RAM) – is just as critical a component in your new computer as the processor. More so, even. Too little memory and the fastest processor in the world will choke on its workload; stacks of memory and you can run several software applications at the same time without the system stuttering, hanging or crashing.

At the simplest level, computer applications run in RAM, by which we mean the files required to open and maintain a given program are transferred from the hard disk, where the program is installed, to RAM for the duration of the session. If you turn off your computer or it crashes, RAM's memory is 'flushed' or wiped out, so you have to start again. That's why it's so very important to save your work as you go along. Only then are your changes copied from RAM back to the hard drive for permanent storage.

Let's say you want to perform a sum in a spreadsheet. The spreadsheet program isolates the data required to perform the sum. RAM then sends this data to the processor. The processor crunches the numbers, comes up with an answer, and sends it back to RAM. Finally, RAM feeds the result to your spreadsheet program and the solution appears on your monitor screen.

It all happens very quickly indeed. However, in all but the most intensive applications, such as real-time video editing, the overall speed of the system is governed far more by RAM than by the processor. When a computer runs painfully slowly, chances are that RAM is the bottleneck, not the processor.

Some memory modules sport their very own heatsinks to help diffuse the heat. Cynics argue that these bolt-on accessories are mainly for show, like go-faster stripes.

QUICK Q&A

How much memory do I really need?

If you're running the 32-bit version of Windows then you're limited to 4GB of memory although, for reasons far too dull to go into, you'll only actually be able to use 3.5GB of that. With the 64-bit version, however, Windows can handle as much RAM as you fancy throwing at it. So how much should you install?

We think that for everyday computing, 4GB is about right: the difference in price between 4GB and 2GB isn't much and the difference in PC performance is quite dramatic. For more intensive tasks, such as high-resolution photo or video editing, 8GB is a sensible amount. We'd advise checking the system requirements for the programs you're likely to use and then at least doubling the specified RAM.

We'd also advise checking the small print, as the quoted figures don't always reflect what you'll need for every feature. For example, using the video features of some photo-editing programs doubles the minimum RAM required and even some word-processing features won't get out of bed for systems that have the minimum memory the system requirements ask for. For example, while Office 2010 says it'll run in 256MB of RAM, it recommends 512MB for 'graphics features and certain advanced functionality' and it also says you'll need 1GB if you want to run OneNote's audio search. Remember that that's over and above the memory that Windows needs and that other programs – anti-virus, music players and so on – require.

If your PC has integrated graphics, it may use some of your system memory as graphics memory – and that means Windows and your various programs won't be able to access it.

Modules

RAM comes in the form of chips soldered to long, thin modules that plug into slots on the motherboard. These modules are remarkably easy to install but buying the right modules in the first place is a more complicated matter.

As mentioned above, any motherboard/chipset supports one type of RAM and one alone. This is not to say that you should buy your motherboard first and then look for compatible memory modules as an afterthought. Quite the reverse, in fact: as soon as you've decided between an Intel or an AMD processor, turn your thoughts to RAM and let this decision govern your choice of chipset (and hence motherboard).

Now, we could fill the rest of this manual with techie talk about memory evolution, error-checking, voltages, transistor counts, latency and so forth, but it would make your eyes glaze over and get us almost nowhere. Let's focus instead on the absolute essentials.

DDR-RAM

Memory chips have come in a variety of standards over the years: SD-RAM, RD-RAM, DDR, DDR2 and DDR3. Unless you're planning to use a fairly old motherboard – and when you consider how cheap modern motherboards are, that's probably a false economy – then the one you need to know about is DDR3. DDR3 stands for Double Data Rate type 3 RAM and it comes in modules known as double inline memory modules – DIMMs for short.

Before DDR RAM came along, memory transferred data according to the motherboard's clock speed; if your clock speed was 200MHz, your memory would be capable of transferring data 200 million times per second. With Double Data Rate (DDR) RAM, however, the memory could send and receive data twice per clock cycle – so in the case of our 200MHz clock speed, it would be transferring data 400 times per second. DDR2 took things a step further and transferred data at four times the clock speed, so to use our 200MHz clock once again we'd be transferring data 800 times per second. The recent DDR3 standard ups the stakes again and shuffles data around at eight times the clock speed, and no doubt there will be a DDR4 standard that doubles that.

There are 184 pins in this DDR DIMM. DDR memory is compatible with both Intel and AMD processors.

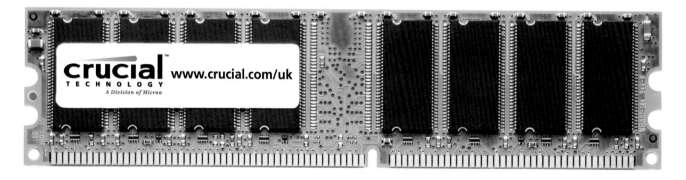

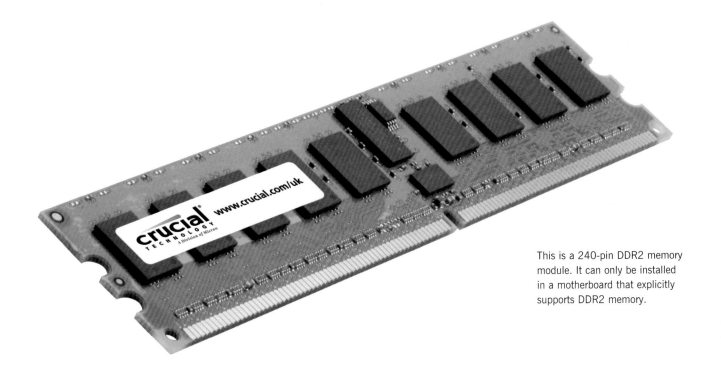

This is a 240-pin DDR2 memory module. It can only be installed in a motherboard that explicitly supports DDR2 memory.

At the time of writing, DDR3 is the one you need to know about: the majority of motherboards now support it, and DDR3 prices have plummeted. While it's still possible to buy DDR2 RAM – there are lots of ageing PCs out there that use it – we think that for current projects, there's precious little point in using it. DDR3 is almost certainly the kind of RAM you'll be putting into your system.

Dual-channel memory

Many motherboards support dual-channel memory configurations. The idea is that you can run two modules in parallel at the same time to effectively double the bandwidth between RAM and the processor, which speeds up your system. The trick is having two memory controllers on the motherboard.

The standard analogy for dual-channel memory is a jammed motorway. Let's say you have three lanes of traffic cruising at 70mph. If you want to get more cars from A to B in a given time, what can you do? Well, first you can increase the traffic flow by raising the speed limit. This is akin to running memory at ever-faster clock speeds. So now you have a three-lane motorway with traffic hurtling along at 140mph. The next option is squeezing more cars into the available space. This is the approach of DDR2 and DDR3. Traffic moves at the same speed – 70mph – but now there's twice as much of it. However, the motorway is now running at full speed with no spare room (or safe distance) between the vehicles. What else can you do to shift more traffic?

You can build an identical motorway alongside the first. This is what a dual-channel memory configuration does. Apply the methodology to a motherboard and in theory it shifts twice as much data to the processor and thus does everything twice as quickly. In practice, the benefits are more modest but it's still an increased performance that you can feel rather than merely chart in a benchmark test.

The critical thing about dual-channelling is that you must use two identical modules and install them in the correct slots. If you try to dual-channel with modules of different speeds or capacities, it will not work.

We'll leave the last word to the respected computing site Tom's Hardware, which tested single- and dual-channel DDR2 memory:

The performance difference between single channel and dual channel DDR2-800 memory using an up-to-date Core 2 Duo system is little to nil. Most tests show differences, but they are really small. For games and enthusiast PCs, we recommend sticking to high-performance dual channel RAM, because the memory is one of those components that you want to perform best for a smooth experience. For regular applications, though, it doesn't really matter much whether you run single or dual channel.

Here's a summary of the current possibilities with DDR, DDR2 and DDR3 memory modules:

Name	Internal clock (MHz)	External memory speed (MHz)	Bus width (bits)	Bandwidth (MB/s)
DDR3-2133	266	1067	64	17,066
DDR3-1866	233	933	64	14,933
DDR3-1600	200	800	64	12,800
DDR3-1333	166	667	64	10,667
DDR3-1066	133	533	64	8,533
DDR3-800	100	400	64	6,400
DDR2-1066	266	533	64	8,533
DDR2-800	200	400	64	6,400
DDR2-667	166	333	64	5,333
DDR2-533	133	267	64	4,266
DDR2-400	100	200	64	3,200

Selecting memory

The first rule of buying memory is to buy the fastest memory that your motherboard supports. For example, if your motherboard supports DDR3 memory running at speeds of 2400MHz, 1866MHz, 1600MHz, 1333MHz, 1066MHz, or 800MHz, you'll get the best performance from memory that runs at 2400Mhz – assuming that you can find it or afford it. The very fastest memory modules can be hard to track down and ruinously expensive.

The motherboard isn't the only part of the picture, however: your processor's memory support matters too; just because a motherboard is capable of communicating with memory at 2400MHz doesn't mean the CPU can. That's why you should always check the processor's full specification before choosing memory. For example, our Core i5 2500K processor supports DDR3-1066/1333 RAM, so there's absolutely no point in paying extra for modules that run faster than 1333MHz.

There is an exception to that, however. XMP (short for Extreme Memory Profile) is designed for overclockers – that is, PC users who know their way around the insides of PCs and who want to fiddle with them to get every last bit of speed. If you're building

a PC around a recent Core i5 or Core i7 processor and your motherboard supports XMP, you can run memory faster. For example, our Core i5 2500K processor supports a maximum speed of 1333MHz, but if it's in an XMP motherboard it can run at 1600MHz. The motherboard we've chosen for our Core i5-powered project is XMP-compatible, which is why we've bought 1600MHz memory rather than 1333MHz memory.

Overclocking is an advanced subject for power users that's beyond the scope of this manual – if you push every component to its maximum possible speed and you don't know what you're doing, there's significant potential for disaster. We think that, for the overwhelming majority of PC builders, XMP is irrelevant and the speed gains negligible. If you stick with the standard memory specifications, your PC will still run perfectly speedily.

Here's a top tip: don't try to match motherboards to specific memory modules yourself. It's much easier to let an online memory chooser, such as Crucial Technology's one (**www.crucial.com/uk**), do the hard work for you. It enables you to enter details of your motherboard and then tells you what memory is compatible with it. Here's how it works.

Visit the Crucial website and, if it isn't already in the middle of the screen, click on Memory Advisor to bring up the memory chooser. Click on the Manufacturer drop-down and then select the manufacturer of your motherboard from the list. If the firm makes laptops and desktops as well as motherboards, you'll be asked which kind of product you're using. Select motherboards and then choose the specific model from the list. Click on Find It to continue.

2

As you can see, Crucial has identified quite a few different options for us, ranging from single 1GB memory modules (around £9 plus VAT) to twin 8GB modules at £190 for the pair. The difference in price is due to two things: memory capacity and memory speed. You'll get a similar selection if you use the memory finder of Crucial's rival, Kingston. Remember that your processor doesn't necessarily support the fastest speeds that your motherboard does.

3

If you look at the smaller print below each option you'll see the specs, so while the yellow-bordered Recommended Upgrade is 16GB of DDR3-1333 memory, there's faster DDR3-1866 memory immediately below it. If you want the fastest memory Crucial makes for this kind of motherboard, that's the one you need – although of course you don't need to go for the fastest, largest chips unless you really have to. For our project we chose an 8GB, DDR3-1600 kit.

PART 2

Case

Just as all motherboards adhere to certain industry-standard dimensions, so too do computer cases. Far and away the most common form factor is, again, ATX. You can be sure that any ATX motherboard will fit in any ATX case. That's the kind of simplicity that we appreciate. But that's not to say that all cases are the same.

Towers vs desktops

Far from it, in fact. For starters, you can choose between a tower case or a desktop case. One is tall and narrow, the other squat and wide. We heartily recommend going for a tower case. They are overwhelmingly more prevalent than desktop cases and, in our experience, considerably easier to work with. The exception would be if you're building a home-entertainment-style PC for living room use. In this case, style matters almost as much as function.

You can get full-sized, mid-sized and mini tower cases, which are progressively shorter versions of the same thing. The sole advantage of a low-rise tower is neatness; the considerable disadvantage is a corresponding lack of expansion possibilities. A mini-tower will typically have two or three 5.25-inch drive bays, a mid-tower between three and five, and a full-tower anywhere up to seven. Given that you will probably install an optical drive,

Here we see a full tower case with a side panel removed and its front fascia on and off.

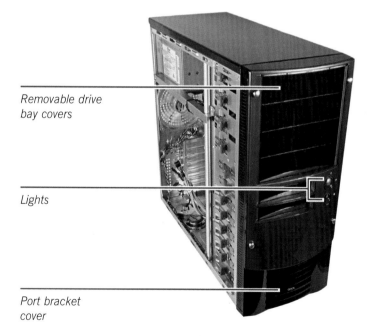

Removable drive bay covers

Lights

Port bracket cover

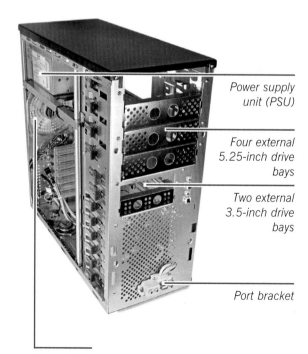

Power supply unit (PSU)

Four external 5.25-inch drive bays

Two external 3.5-inch drive bays

Port bracket

Internal fan

Aluminium cases like this one from Lian-Li are light, strong and cool.

a three-bay case still has room for two further devices (such as sound card breakout boxes).

Pay attention to 3.5-inch drive bays too, as that's where you'll put the hard disk. In our projects we'll install a single, very large hard disk, but if you think you might want to add more than one later on or take advantage of technologies such as RAID (more of that in a moment) then it's a good idea to ensure there are sufficient drive bays.

In short, you want to allow your PC room to grow. Of course, it's always possible to strip the entire innards from a computer and reinstall everything in a larger case should the need arise, but this is about the most drastic and fiddly upgrade you could ever perform. Better, we suggest, to allow for future expansion at the outset.

A non-ATX small form factor platform like this offers little in the way of expansion possibilities, but you may consider that a fair compromise if you need a looker for the living room.

Case features

Drive bays are protected by drive bay covers on the front of the case. These snap-out or unscrew to afford full access to the bay, whereupon you can install an internally-mounted drive.

A case also has a series of blanking plates to the rear that correspond to the motherboard's expansion slots. You'll remove one every time you install an expansion card. Above this is a rectangular input-output (I/O) panel. This is where the mouse, keyboard, parallel and other ports poke through when the motherboard is installed.

On the front of the case, you will find two buttons: the main power on/off switch and a smaller, usually recessed reset button that restarts your computer if Windows hangs. There will be a couple of lights, too: one to show when the power is on and one that flickers whenever the hard disk drive is particularly active. The case may also have an extra opening to accommodate an expansion bracket loaded with audio or USB ports.

Your case may have a single all-encompassing cover that lifts straight off or separate removable side panels. It may be held together with screws, thumbscrews or some arrangement of clips. Internally, you may find a removable motherboard tray. This is a boon, as it's much easier to install the motherboard on an external tray than it is to fiddle around inside the case.

Inside the case, along with the drive bays and a cluster of cables, you'll find a pre-installed fan or two and possibly a mounting area for an optional extra fan. The case will also have a speaker which the BIOS will use to generate beeps (see p.158).

Beyond all of this, designs vary from the standard, boring 'big beige box' look to undeniably funky. Pressed-steel cases are generally cheaper but brushed-aluminium looks (and stays) cooler. Some cases are heavy, reinforced and thoroughly sturdy; others are lightweight, flimsy and easily dented. We would simply advise you to focus on functionality before frills. A full-sized tower case is generally easier to work with, easier to keep tidy internally, more adaptable to customisation and provides better airflow to the motherboard's components.

The same case we saw a moment ago, stripped of its covers and seen from the rear.

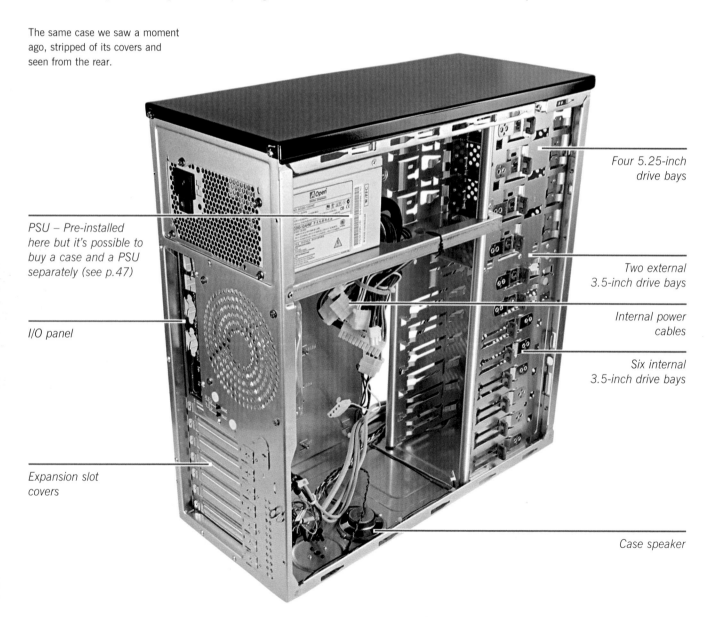

PSU – Pre-installed here but it's possible to buy a case and a PSU separately (see p.47)

I/O panel

Expansion slot covers

Four 5.25-inch drive bays

Two external 3.5-inch drive bays

Internal power cables

Six internal 3.5-inch drive bays

Case speaker

PART  # Power supply unit

The power supply unit (PSU), as the name suggests, supplies power to your PC. However, all PSUs are not created equal, so don't just assume that any old PSU will work well in your PC. Many cases come with a PSU installed, which can be a big time saver, but whether you buy a separate PSU or go for one that comes inside a case, it's important to ensure that the one you get will be up to the job.

Compatibility

To go with your ATX case and ATX motherboard, you need an ATX PSU. Virtually all new PSUs comply with the ATX standard, which means it will fit in an ATX case and power an ATX motherboard.

A reliable power supply unit is a must. This ATX model has an adjustable fan speed for quiet running and pumps out 350W.

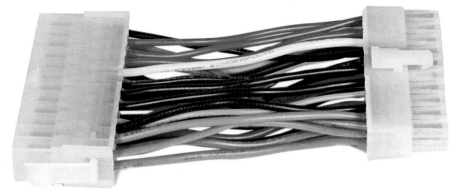

An adapter for converting a 24-pin PSU connector to a 20-pin motherboard.

However, if you are using a recent Intel processor and motherboard, take care. You'll need one of the newer PSUs that has a 24-pin power connector rather than the older 20-pin standard. If you intend to reuse an older PSU or if you buy a 20-pin unit and later find that you can't connect it to your motherboard, all is not lost: you can buy an adapter to convert a 20-pin connector to a 24-pin connector. However, this is not advisable unless the PSU pumps out at least 450W of power. We strongly recommend that you buy a new 24-pin PSU instead. Conversely, though, you can also get an adapter to convert a new 24-pin PSU for use with an older 20-pin motherboard, and that's risk-free.

Also ensure that you get a PSU with SATA connectors if you have a SATA-enabled motherboard and SATA hard drives. Again, an adapter or two can save the day but it is better to buy the appropriate equipment in the first place.

We don't recommend buying a second-hand PSU. An under-powered PSU might not supply power-hungry components with the juice they need, particularly if you cram your case full of drives and accessories, and an older unit with a history of hard work behind it is obviously more liable to burn out and die.

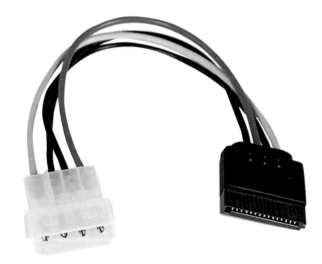

An IDE-to-SATA adapter for powering new-style drives from an older PSU.

Yet another adapter. This one converts a Molex cable into a pair of SATA connectors.

Power rating

A 250W or 300W power supply will probably be inadequate, but a 700W will probably be overkill unless you're running a very powerful processor and graphics card. Check the specifications of your chosen processor and graphics card to make sure your chosen PSU has enough puff to power them.

Cooling

A PSU has an integrated fan that controls airflow through the computer case. Some also have a second fan that blows cool air at the motherboard. We strongly recommend that you buy a PSU specifically rated for the kind of processor you intend to use.

Noise

A secondary consideration, certainly, but important nonetheless. Some PSUs make a terrible racket while others operate with barely a whisper. If a peaceful PC is important to you, shop around for a quiet device with adjustable-speed fans. See also Appendix 1.

Connectors

The PSU connects directly to each internal drive in your PC and to the motherboard itself, supplying the lot with power. Here's a run through of what to expect.

ATX power The main power connector that plugs directly into the motherboard. As mentioned above, the design has switched recently from 20-pin plugs to 24-pin.

ATX Auxiliary A secondary 6-pin power connection required by some older motherboards. If your motherboard has an ATX Auxiliary socket, you must connect this cable.

ATX 12V Some Pentium 4 motherboards require yet another cable connection from the PSU to provide extra power to the processor. However, the latest Socket 775 motherboards dispense with this.

Molex drive connector Used to power hard disk and optical drives.

SATA drive connector Used to power Serial ATA hard drives (and some of the latest optical drives).

Berg drive connector Used primarily to power the floppy drive.

PART 2

Hard disk drive

In recent years, hard disks have grown dramatically in size – which is just as well, because the amount of storage space the average PC user needs has increased dramatically too. Digital media – that is, photos, music and video – are the worst offenders; for example, if you're using a high-definition video camcorder, a two-minute clip takes around 200MB of space. That's a fifth of a gigabyte!

You can of course add extra storage later – if your PC has a spare USB port you can easily connect an external hard disk – but it's cheaper to buy a bigger hard disk when you build your PC than to skimp on storage now and have to buy more in the not-too-distant future. The good news is that hard disks with capacities of 500GB or more have plummeted in price and they're cheap enough to consider for your home-made PC project.

A hard disk drive stores data on high-speed spinning magnetic platters. Remarkably, they last for tens of thousands of hours.

Interface

There's more to a hard disk than how much storage space it has. Its interface matters too, because that will dictate the speed at which your PC can transfer data to and from the disk as well as what kind of disk you can buy. Modern motherboards tend to come with multiple Serial ATA (SATA) connections, which replace the older IDE (Integrated Drive Electronics) and ATA (Advanced Technology Attachment) interfaces. SATA is the better technology: it's faster, simpler and considerably less fiddly to install, and its diminutive cables mean it's better for air circulation too.

Here is how the different standards shape up:

Interface	Also known as	Maximum bandwidth (MB/s)
ATA-66	ATA-5, IDE-66 or UDMA-66	66
ATA-100	ATA-6, IDE-100 or UDMA-100	100
ATA-133	ATA-7, IDE-133 or UDMA-133	133
SATA-150	SATA I	150
SATA-300	SATA II	300
SATA-600	SATA III	600

A 40-conductor IDE/ATA cable, an 80-conductor IDE/ATA cable, and a SATA cable.

Data transfer rates

The real-word performance of a drive isn't just dependent on the bandwidth: the specification that really matters is called the 'sustained data transfer rate', which tells you how quickly the drive can read data from its own disk before transferring it across the interface. Manufacturers are notoriously shifty about sustained data transfer rates as they're often significantly lower than the headline-grabbing maximum interface speeds. For example, while a SATA III drive is theoretically capable of transferring 600MB per second, sustained data transfer rates of around 125MB per second aren't unusual. That doesn't mean you shouldn't use the fastest connectors available, though: such drives are capable of faster speeds, albeit for shorter periods.

Cables

Before SATA became the standard way to connect hard disks and other storage, this section was much longer. SATA devices simply need a single SATA cable between them and the motherboard, plus a power source. And that's it.

eSATA

There's one more standard worth knowing, and that's eSATA. The 'e' stands for 'external' and eSATA is a standard high-speed connection for external storage devices. It's not the only way to connect external drives – USB and FireWire connectors can be used too – but it's much faster than the other standards.

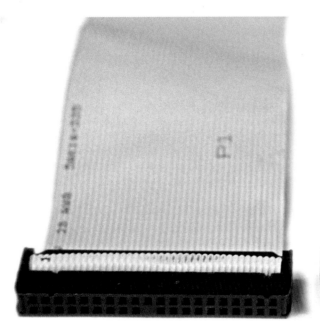

Other things to think about

Cache   A drive's cache is a little bit of memory that it uses to store frequently accessed data, saving a little bit of time each time that data is accessed. A 2MB cache is okay, but 8MB is much better. Some really large drives have caches as large as 64MB.

Speed   We've mentioned data transfer speeds, but the speed at which a drive spins is important too. All other things being equal, a drive that spins at 7200rpm should have a faster data transfer rate than a drive that spins at 5400rpm.

SMART   SMART drives include clever error checkers that keep an eye on the hard disk for signs of damage and can sometimes predict imminent failure. Even if your drive has SMART technology, though, don't rely on it: work on the assumption that one day your hard disk will fail and make sure you keep regular backups of anything important.

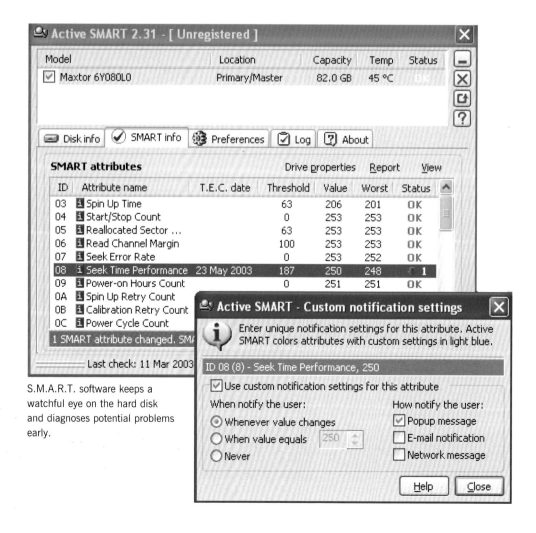

S.M.A.R.T. software keeps a watchful eye on the hard disk and diagnoses potential problems early.

Hard disks such as Seagate's Barracuda can have caches as large as 64MB to speed up access to frequently used data.

RAID

Hard disks can and do fail, and one way to ensure that such failures don't take any important data with them is to use a system known as RAID. RAID stands for Redundant Array of Independent Disks (it used to be 'inexpensive' disks, but that fell out of favour) and lets you use two or more hard disks simultaneously to 'stripe' or 'mirror' data. Many motherboards support RAID, and Windows does too.

There are several kinds of RAID storage in common use. The simplest kind is RAID Level 0, which 'stripes': that is, it treats multiple hard disks as one really big one, so for example it would see two 100MB drives as if they were one 200MB drive. By distributing data evenly between the drives, RAID can deliver better performance but there's no redundancy with this method: if one drive fails, tough luck.

RAID Level 1 uses mirroring instead of striping, so whatever is stored on drive 1 is copied to drive 2. It's a fairly expensive way to protect your data, but it does work very well: if drive 1 fails, all your stuff is still accessible on drive 2.

The plummeting cost of recordable DVD discs and external drives and the rise of cloud-based backup services means that RAID is probably overkill for home use, but for critical business data it's a very effective tool.

PART 2 Sound card

If you want to play music, enjoy films, watch YouTube clips, make your own movies or enjoy PC games, then some kind of sound system is a must. Most motherboards now come with integrated audio but you can choose from a selection of add-on sound cards that promise to delight even the most exacting ears.

Stereo or surround sound?

Audio comes in two main flavours: stereo, which is designed to be played through two speakers, and surround, which is designed to be played through three or more speakers. Surround sound systems are described in the format X.1, where X is the number of speakers and '.1' is a subwoofer that delivers a low-end thump. For example, a 2.1 surround system has two speakers and a subwoofer; a 5.1 system five and a subwoofer, and a 7.1 system seven speakers and a subwoofer. For music, surround sound is overkill but it's great for films and games.

The negatives are price and space: good quality surround speakers can be expensive and they need to be spread around the room if you want to get the full effect. For example, a 5.1 surround sound system is designed to have one speaker at the TV or monitor, one on either side, and two more behind you.

If you think you'll want to use surround sound, make sure your motherboard's built-in audio supports the kind of surround sound you want to use or invest in an add-on sound card that does.

Logitech's Z906 speaker system sounds phenomenal but it isn't cheap: expect to pay around £329.

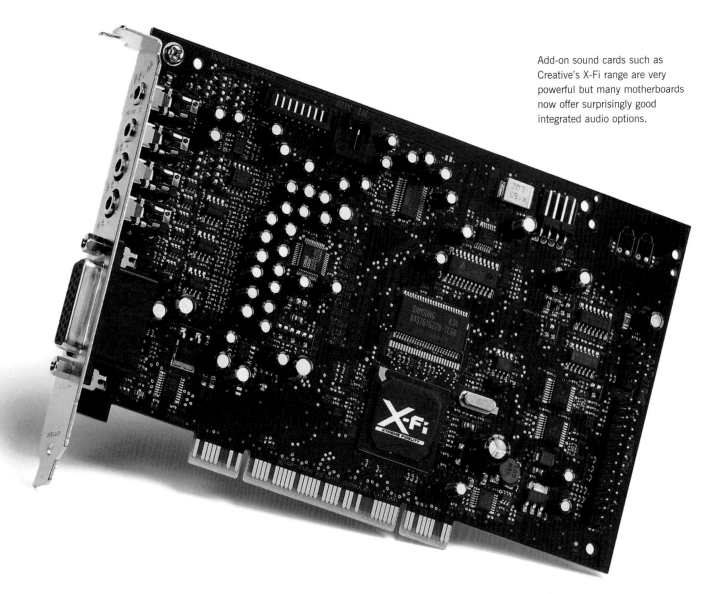

Add-on sound cards such as Creative's X-Fi range are very powerful but many motherboards now offer surprisingly good integrated audio options.

When space is tight, sound ports typically double up duties. Two of the three ports here (lower right corner) function either as speaker outputs or as line and mic inputs, depending upon how the audio driver software is currently configured.

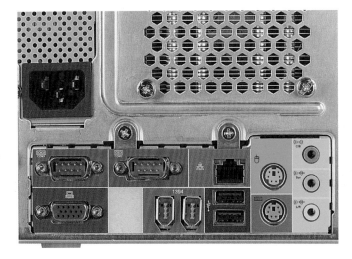

Integrated or expansion card?

If all you want to hear is the odd beep from Windows and the occasional music track, then there's no point buying an additional sound card if your motherboard already includes integrated audio. However, if you intend to use good-quality speakers for high-quality music or movie soundtracks, then a dedicated sound card may offer superior performance.

Keen gamers may prefer stand-alone sound cards too: firms such as Creative pride themselves on making sound cards that game developers can use to create really immersive soundtracks.

Our advice? Unless you're an audiophile or the motherboard doesn't do what you want to do, give your motherboard's integrated audio a go before spending money on any more components. You might be pleasantly surprised by the sounds your motherboard can make – especially if you aren't using very expensive, very detailed speakers.

PART 2 **Video card**

Today's graphics cards are more powerful than the PCs of just a few years ago and they're capable of astonishing things. Inevitably they're also capable of being rather confusing. Let's make some sense of it all.

GPUs and graphics memory

Graphics cards are essentially little computers in their own right, with dedicated GPUs (graphics processing units) supported by a hefty chunk of dedicated video memory. The Radeon card (pictured) runs at 925MHz, has 3GB of on-board GDDR5 graphics memory and boasts a dizzying array of statistics including '3.79 TFLOPS Single Precision Compute Power'. At the time of writing it's also the best part of four hundred quid.

A graphics card's job is to put pictures on your PC's screen but there are enormous differences between the cheapest and most expensive ones. Cutting-edge cards are capable of almost photorealistic images. They can create those images in real time and animate them so quickly you can't see any delays. More modest cards may struggle with anything more complicated than the Windows Desktop.

So what do you actually need? For Windows, we'd recommend a graphics card with at least 256MB of on-board memory and support for at least version 10 of Microsoft's DirectX graphics technology. If you intend to play lots of 3D games, go for something even more powerful: 1GB or more. By 3D, we don't mean funny-glasses 3D, although many modern graphics cards are capable of that if you have 3D glasses; we mean games that give the impression of being three-dimensional by using very realistic graphics.

It looks like a spaceship, but this is a Radeon HD graphics card from AMD. It's more powerful than our car.

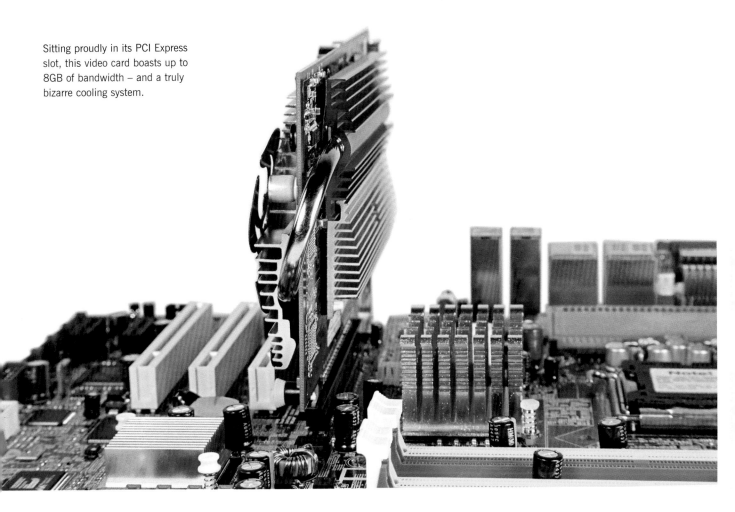

Sitting proudly in its PCI Express slot, this video card boasts up to 8GB of bandwidth – and a truly bizarre cooling system.

Interface

Graphics card interfaces have evolved quite considerably in recent years: PCI cards were usurped by AGP (Accelerated Graphics Port) cards, which in turn have been usurped by PCI Express (PCIe) cards. While early PCIe cards were hilariously expensive, prices have plummeted as choice has widened. As a result, PCIe is the standard to look for, as everything from £18 cheapies to high-end, several-hundred-pound graphics cards use the technology.

Even if you intend to use a motherboard's integrated graphics system, it's a very good idea to ensure that the board also has a PCIe slot: if you decide a year or two down the line that you'd really like a better graphics processor and the motherboard does not have a PCIe slot, you'll have to throw it out and buy a new one. Doing that can be an enormous pain and might involve having to buy other components such as memory modules. Unless you're absolutely certain that you'll never, ever need any more graphics power than the integrated solution your motherboard offers, make sure your chosen board has room for a stand-alone PCIe card.

Connections

Modern graphics cards tend to have multiple connections for monitors and TVs, although unless the cards are specifically designed to run multiple monitors simultaneously the connectors can't be used simultaneously. The most common connectors you'll find on the back of a graphics card are VGA, DVI and HDMI.

VGA (Video Graphics Array) is the oldest standard and it's an analogue one: your graphics card takes digital information, turns it into an analogue signal and transmits it across the cable. That was fine in the days of analogue cathode ray tube displays, but today's monitors are digital – so they have to turn the VGA data back into digital data. Whenever there's conversion from analogue to digital there's the potential for data loss and analogue cables can also suffer from interference if they aren't shielded properly.

DVI (Digital Video Interface) is a better option because, as the name suggests, it's digital – so there's no conversion going on and therefore no risk of data loss or interference. Picture quality is better and the graphics card and the monitor work as a team to give you the best possible results.

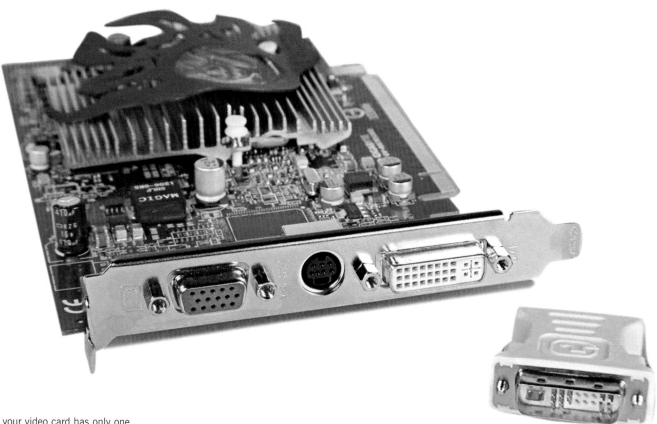

If your video card has only one port, make sure that it's DVI. This one also has VGA, which is handy, but the alternative is a DVI-to-VGA adapter.

Another new standard is HDMI (High Definition Multimedia Interface). Like DVI, it's digital but, unlike DVI, it can also carry audio. As a result it's the connection of choice for modern home entertainment equipment such as flat-screen TVs, Blu-Ray players and so on, although most graphics cards' HDMI ports only export video, not audio, so you will probably also need a separate cable to connect your PC's audio outputs to your TV or sound system.

Depending on the kind of card you buy, you might encounter other options too. Some graphics cards have S-Video or Composite Video connections to link up with other video equipment, while TV tuner cards have a connector for a TV aerial or satellite cable so you can use your PC to watch and record TV. Cards are also available with video-in connections so you can digitise old video, although for modern camcorders you're more likely to connect the camcorder to a USB port and transfer footage that way.

Last but not least there's DisplayPort, which hasn't really taken the world by storm just yet: you'll find it in some high-end and 3D-capable graphics cards. Ultimately it hopes to displace DVI. For now, though, it remains relatively uncommon.

If you're connecting your PC to a monitor, look for a video card with DVI outputs; if you're going to connect it to a TV, look for one with HDMI. Of course, there's nothing to stop you buying a card that has both. Many do.

QUICK Q&A

My video card has both VGA and DVI ports. Can I connect two monitors?

Probably not. Many video cards provide two outputs but these are mere alternatives i.e. you can use one port or the other but not both simultaneously. If you want to run two monitors, the usual approach is to install a PCI video card alongside the AGP card and connect one monitor to each. Windows recognises this arrangement automatically so configuration is straightforward.

However, you can also get 'dual-head' and 'triple-head' video cards that incorporate all the circuitry required to run two or three monitors through the same bus.

Some graphics cards can run twin monitors simultaneously, but most can't. Make sure you check the specs.

A quick word about cables

When we needed a new HDMI cable for our PC recently we popped into a well known electronics retailer to buy one – but we left empty-handed because they wanted £89.99 for it. You can buy exactly the same kind of cable from a no-name manufacturer for £8.99 and even that's quite pricey for what's ultimately six feet of wire with a very simple plug on either end.

So what do you get for the extra £81? The short answer is 'nothing'.

The long answer is also 'nothing'. According to electronics retailer Kogan, 'An HDMI cable is an HDMI cable. It's a digital cable. You either get a picture or you don't. Don't get conned into buying a "fancy" HDMI cable because it will make no difference.'

Remember that we're talking about digital signals here and digital signals are binary: data is either a zero or a one; there are no other possibilities. Cables can transmit those zeros and ones but they can't improve on them: an expensive cable won't make the zeros more zero-y or the ones more one-y and a cheap cable won't transmit half a zero or six-eighths of a one. Binary is either on or off. It's never slightly on or a little bit off.

There are some circumstances in which slightly more expensive cables do make a difference, but those circumstances are when you're running cables over exceptionally long distances through powerful electromagnetic fields, which doesn't describe very many home entertainment setups. Cheap cables are certainly more likely to fail completely than more expensive, better made ones, so it's not a bad idea to get something reasonably well made and well shielded if you're running it behind a wall with the intention of plastering over the top of it, but even then £80 is far too much. Build quality is only really an issue if you're constantly moving your cables about, unplugging them and plugging them back in.

Don't just take our word for it. All kinds of sites and publications – *Expert Reviews*, Tested.com, CNet and so on – have tested ludicrously expensive cables against cheap ones and found absolutely no difference in picture quality between the cheapest and the most expensive products. HDMI is a standard; if a cable is HDMI compliant then it shouldn't and generally doesn't make the slightest bit of difference if it costs £8 or £80.

Copy protection and HD video

The ongoing war on internet piracy means that there's an acronym you need to know about if you intend to watch high-definition films on your PC: HDCP, which is short for High-bandwidth Digital Content Protection. Films on Blu-Ray discs and downloads from the likes of Apple's iTunes Store are examples of HDCP content. If you don't have the right components, they won't play properly. That means you need an HDCP-compliant graphics card, an HDCP-compliant display or TV, and you need to connect them via an HDCP-compliant DVI or HDMI cable. A VGA cable can't be HDCP compliant as it isn't digital.

The idea behind HDCP is to prevent pirates from making pristine digital copies of high-definition films. Of course, it hasn't stopped them in the slightest – however, it has caused headaches for ordinary PC users. That's because HDCP expects the Blu-Ray drive (if used), graphics card, cable and monitor all to be HDCP compliant. If any point in the chain doesn't identify itself as HDCP compliant, then you don't get a high-definition picture.

CHOOSING YOUR HARDWARE

Optical drives

Most PCs you'll see in the shops come with some kind of optical drive, such as a CD or DVD drive or a Blu-Ray drive, and many of them can create such discs as well as play them. Digital distribution of music, films and software means that the days of the optical disc are probably numbered but it's got a good few years left in it yet – and without an optical drive, you can't convert your CDs to digital music or play Blu-Ray movie discs.

Interface

Until fairly recently optical drives used IDE/ATA interfaces but recent motherboards much prefer the simpler, faster Serial ATA (SATA) connectors we've already encountered in hard disk drives. We'd definitely advise you to get a SATA drive: there's no messing around with fiddly switches or settings; all you do is plug one end of the data cable into the drive and the other end into the motherboard. It doesn't get much easier than that. Older optical drives wouldn't play audio until you ran a separate cable from the drive to the PC's motherboard or sound card but SATA drives don't have that hurdle.

There are two other good reasons to buy SATA now: the relative lack of cabling helps keep the inside of your PC cool and, even if your current motherboard is happy with IDE/ATA drives, your next one probably won't be.

Modern drives can handle all kinds of discs: this one from Liteon plays CDs, DVDs and Blu-Ray discs; it can record CDs and DVDs too.

CD discs

A plain CD drive can play music and data CDs. If it's a CD-RW drive, it can also create music or data CDs. There are two kinds of recordable CD: CD-R (Compact Disc Recordable) and CR-RW (Compact Disc Rewritable). A recordable CD can be used to record just once – once you've done that, you can't record on it again. That makes it quite good for making CD compilations for the car or CDs full of photos to send to the in-laws but it's not ideal for storing files. CD-RW is a better option, as you can record, erase, record, erase and keep on recording and erasing for as long as you like (or for as long as the CD lasts). That makes CD-RW useful for additional file storage.

The problem with CD-R and CD-RW is that they aren't particularly roomy: you get 700MB to 800MB of storage, which in these days of high-resolution photos and high-definition video isn't very much. If you need to store more data, the next step up is the much roomier DVD.

Recordable DVD discs

DVDs aren't just for watching films, although of course they're quite good for that too. DVDs also provide very large amounts of storage: gigabytes compared to the megabytes on a CD. Unfortunately, things are a little bit more confusing than they need to be, because there are three recordable DVD formats: DVD-R/-RW (the 'minus formats'), DVD+R/RW (the 'plus formats'), and DVD-RAM.

For most of us, there is no difference between the plus formats and the minus ones: DVD+R/+RW discs have minor technical differences compared to DVD-R/-RW ones, but they're insignificant to you and to us. Most modern drives support both the plus and minus formats, so it doesn't really matter anyway. What does matter is the different kinds of disc. As with CDs, R means recordable, so a DVD-R disc can be recorded on once, and RW means rewritable. A RAM disc is another kind of rewritable disc that's only supported by certain manufacturers.

What does this mean for you?

- If you want to backup important files, any of the formats will work just fine. DVD-R discs are by far the cheapest ones to buy, so backing up to one-time DVD-R is the cheapest way to store lots of stuff.
- If you want to make DVD movie discs to watch on a normal DVD player, DVD-R is more compatible than DVD+R. Few DVD players can play DVD-RAM discs.
- If you want to store data, a drive that supports +R/RW dual-layer discs is a smart choice. Single-layer DVDs give you 4.7GB of storage, but dual-layer ones double that to a very healthy 8.5GB. That means more data per disc, which makes backing up data less of a hassle. Double-sided, dual-layer discs are bigger still, with up to 17GB of storage per disc.

DVD and CD technology are very similar, so if you get a drive that can burn DVDs, it will also be able to create CDs.

Blu-Ray discs

Things change quickly in technology: in the third edition of this book we reported that two contenders wanted to replace DVD: HD-DVD and Blu-Ray. HD-DVD is now dead and Blu-Ray is well established, although it hasn't quite replaced DVD and probably

Blu-Ray offers much more storage than standard DVD format and drives can now handle both formats.

won't. It's used primarily for high-definition films and for storing even more data than DVD discs can handle.

Blu-Ray prices have fallen dramatically and it's now possible to get a CD–DVD–Blu-Ray drive for very little money, and that's the option we'd recommend: the savings involved in buying a non-Blu-Ray drive are now negligible. It's worth noting that Blu-Ray discs work slightly differently to CDs and DVDs – they use a blue laser, not the red laser of other disc formats – and as a result, a drive that burns CDs and DVDs isn't necessarily capable of burning Blu-Ray discs too. Many drives, including the ones we've chosen for our PC projects, can burn all three kinds of disc, however.

Inevitably, there are more acronyms to learn. BD-R means recordable Blu-Ray and, again, they're one-time discs. Instead of BD-RW, though, the name for rewritable Blu-Rays is BD-RE.

Drive speeds

Every disc drive has a speed rating for its various functions: CD reading and writing; DVD reading and writing; and – if appropriate – Blu-Ray reading and writing. Speeds are expressed in multiples, so for example you might see a CD drive that's a 48x drive. That means it runs at 48 times the speed of an original CD drive, which ran at 150 kilobytes per second, so a 48x read speed equates to 7200KBps – about 7 megabytes per second. Drives can usually read data much more quickly than they can record it, so for example a CD drive might read at 48x speeds but record to CD-RW discs at a more leisurely 24x.

The multiples aren't carried across different kinds of disc, so for example a 1x DVD drive has a transfer rate almost ten times that of a 1x CD: it throws data around at 1352KBps, which is the equivalent of a 9x CD. A 16x speed DVD drive transfers data at 21MBps. Blu-Ray discs are faster still: a 1x Blu-Ray drive transfers data at 4.5MBps, rising to 54MBps for a 12x drive.

Do these speeds matter? They do if you're transferring lots of data: the faster the drive, the more quickly you can back up files or create CDs. However, as drives rely on spinning discs around at very high speeds there can be problems with some of the fastest devices: the phenomenon of 'disc shattering' can occur at speeds beyond 48x (for CDs), with discs breaking into lots of pieces and ruining both disc and drive. While modern drives have been designed to make shattering very unlikely, if you want the very fastest performance it's probably a good idea to avoid the very cheapest, unbranded blank discs.

Care and feeding

Nothing lasts forever, not even an optical disc. The phrase 'disc rot' describes the way in which a CD, DVD or Blu-Ray disc can become unusable due to chemical issues such as oxidation and ultraviolet light damage, or the much more common physical scuffing and abrasion you get if you don't look after discs properly. If a file, photo or video clip is important to you, don't store it on a single disc.

PART  **Other possibilities**

There's no shortage of potential add-ons and optional extras for a fledgling computer. Here we discuss a few essentials and suggest some other possibilities.

Modem

Before broadband internet access became widely available, a modem was a must-have – you couldn't get online without it. However, these days broadband is cheaper and much, much faster than old-fashioned dial-up internet access; as a result, the only time you need a traditional modem is if you live in a remote bit of the country where broadband isn't available.

If you get broadband, you might still get a modem – a cable modem for cable broadband or an ADSL modem for telephone line broadband – but they're not really modems as we know them; they're usually devices that plug into a spare USB port and connect to your broadband socket in the wall. In most cases you get them free when you sign up with a broadband Internet Service Provider.

A DSL or cable modem will generally be supplied as part of any broadband internet deal but you may need to install your own analogue modem for dial-up internet access.

Wireless networking (Wi-Fi)

If you want to connect PCs without running network cables everywhere, Wi-Fi – wireless networking – can cut the clutter. This is essentially Ethernet without wires, and there are four main standards: 802.11a, b, g and n.

802.11b is the most widely supported standard, but it's also the slowest, with a theoretical maximum speed of 11Mb/sec. 802.11g is faster at 54Mb/sec and also supports the slower 802.11b kit; and 802.11n is faster still, delivering speeds in excess of 100Mb/sec. It has better range, too, and it's less prone to interference. Last and definitely least there's 802.11a, which runs at 54Mb/sec but won't play nicely with the other 802.11 standards.

Many motherboards now include built-in Wi-Fi, usually 802.11b and 802.11g.

There are four key Wi-Fi standards. 802.11n is the fastest and it's usually backwards compatible with older equipment.

FireWire (IEEE-1394)

FireWire is a high-speed (50MB/sec) interface particularly suited to transferring digital video from camcorder to computer or for connecting fast external drives. Need we say that FireWire is increasingly supported by motherboards?

It's an Apple trademark but FireWire works just as well on a PC as a Mac. If your motherboard comes up short, install a PCI expansion card.

Card reader

Everything's digital these days, and if you want to transfer photos or videos from your digital camera, smartphone, tablet or other gadget you have two choices: surround yourself with a stack of USB cables and power adapters, or use a card reader to transfer data directly from the device's memory card. There are two key kinds of card reader: external readers, like the one pictured, and internal ones. We'd recommend an external card reader: they're very, very cheap and don't require any installation, as they simply connect to a spare USB port.

And the rest ...

A mouse, keyboard and monitor are definite givens, and a printer and scanner are obvious peripherals. But how else might you augment your PC?

Headphones and microphone Listen to music or games and record your own voice – or anything else – with a microphone. Windows has a sound recorder built-in but your sound card's software is likely to be more advanced. For use with speech recognition software, the best bet is a quality headset with an earpiece and microphone combined.

Joystick or games controller These usually connect via a USB port but you can also get cordless models for greater flexibility.

A multi-card reader will save you a lot of effort if you've got cameras, smartphones and other gadgets with data to transfer.

Games controllers come in all shapes and sizes, from a simple joystick to this (whatever it may be).

This PCI expansion card provides SATA sockets for additional hard drives.

IDE or SATA controller card Add extra channels to your motherboard and connect another couple of hard disk drives. Essential for RAID, unless your motherboard provides native RAID support, and handy for massive storage requirements.

UPS (Uninterruptible Power Supply) Protect your files from power cuts with a UPS. Basically, it's a mini-generator that kicks in when the lights go out.

If the lights go out unexpectedly, will your data go with them? Not if you invest in a UPS.

Bluetooth A Bluetooth adapter lets your computer 'talk' to and exchange files wirelessly with other Bluetooth-enabled devices, notably mobile phones and PDAs.

PART **Choosing components for the perfect PC**

We're going to build two computers from scratch: a very powerful, expandable full-sized PC in a standard tower case and a smaller, quieter PC for home entertainment applications, such as the BBC iPlayer and watching DVDs and Blu-Ray discs. As we'll discover the process of actually building a PC is very simple: choosing the components is the hard bit!

Pick a processor

The relentless march of technology means that massively powerful quad-core processors are now affordable, even for budget builders. If you want to use your PC for video editing, gaming or other similarly demanding tasks it's definitely worth going for a four-core processor. Don't assume you need the very fastest ones, however. There's a sweet spot when you're buying PC components, and that spot is roughly in the middle of a product range: for example, the Intel processor range currently features the Core i3, Core i5 and Core i7, all of which are blisteringly fast. Our pick would be the Core i5.

The Core i5 is not as quick as the more powerful Core i7 but that doesn't mean it's slow: if they were cars, the i5 would be a fast Ferrari and the i7 an even faster Ferrari. That means the Core i5 delivers exceptionally good performance without a frightening price tag. At the time of writing, you can pick up a very, very fast Core i5 for around £165, while the fastest Core i7 processor retails for more than £800. In everyday use, you wouldn't see any significant difference in the performance of your PC, but you'd certainly feel the difference in your wallet.

Our first PC is designed for really intensive tasks such as video editing and gaming, but if you're building a PC for the living room then you certainly don't need as much horsepower as you do for cutting-edge games. A processor that's designed to handle the graphics, such as AMD's three- and four-core Llano processors, can save quite a lot of money while delivering plenty of performance for high-definition video.

Remember that the choice of processor dictates the kind of motherboard you can use: you can't put Intel processors on motherboards designed for AMD processors or vice versa. When you decide on a processor, check its specification to find out what kind of socket it requires. That's the socket your motherboard will need to have too.

Choose the memory

Unless you're on the tightest of tight budgets, DDR3 memory is the RAM you need for your PC. The more the merrier: 2GB is the lowest you can really get away with, while 4GB is considered adequate for everyday computing. If you're going to be working your PC very hard and your chosen motherboard has enough room, stick 8GB in there. It won't cost significantly more, but you'll be glad you did it, this time next year.

Think about storage

Files expand to fill the space available to them, so don't skimp on storage: if you think 500GB is more space than you'll ever need, take that number and double it. Massive digital photos and high-definition videos take up enormous amounts of hard disk space, and the price of storage is very, very low unless you're considering a solid-state disk. On the subject of which...

If you want the fastest PC possible, don't think about hard disks: think about solid-state drives (SSDs) instead. They're effectively flash memory pretending to be a hard disk and, because there are no moving parts, they're lightning fast. You'll find SSDs in smartphones, iPads and ultra-thin laptops and they really are incredibly quick. Unfortunately they're also incredibly expensive and fairly small: at the time of writing a 256GB SSD is over £300, whereas a traditional hard disk with four times the capacity is about £60. Some power users install two drives in their PCs: an SSD with Windows and important applications on it and a traditional hard disk for file storage. It works very well and makes PCs run very quickly, but for now the costs outweigh the real-world benefits. Give it a few years, however, and SSD storage will be in most PCs.

Choose integrated sound and graphics

If you want to play the very latest games at the very highest quality settings, you'll need a stand-alone graphics card – but motherboard and processor pairings that use built-in, 'integrated' graphics are perfectly capable of decoding high-definition video without breaking sweat. Integrated graphics are cheaper because you don't need to buy a separate graphics card. They also mean you can get away with a less powerful power supply.

Choose the form factor

ATX and a tower case is the Ford Focus of computing: it's widely available and easy to use. We'll use an ATX case for our bigger PC and a smaller Micro ATX motherboard for our home entertainment machine.

Think about where you're going to put it

Before you make the final decisions on your PC, it's worth having a bit of a think about where it's going to live. If it's going to sit on top of or underneath a desk then there are few limitations on what you build, but if you want to build something that fits in the TV unit and doesn't look odd then you might need to shop around for a case that will fit and a motherboard that will fit in the case. Think about networking, too: will the PC be close enough to your broadband router for you to run a cable to it or will you be connecting via Wi-Fi wireless networking?

The other thing to think about is what you're likely to use your PC for. If you plan to use your PC for home entertainment then it's a good idea to think about the connections you'll need, such as audio connections for home cinema speakers or an HDMI port so you can connect your PC to a flat-screen TV. If you want to use your PC as a digital video recorder, you'll need to invest in a TV tuner card and you'll need to connect the tuner to your aerial or satellite dish.

As with all PC building, don't just think about what you're going to do now: think about what you're going to do in the future too. Are you likely to connect your digital camera, camcorder or iPod to your PC? A case with USB ports on the front will make that much easier. Will you want to install additional hardware, such as another hard disk or a TV tuner card? It might be a good idea to pick a case that has sufficient extra room for those components.

Don't forget about peripherals

In addition to the PC itself, you'll need a keyboard, a mouse and a monitor. We're quite keen on Logitech keyboards and mice and BenQ LED monitors, all of which offer decent design and performance at budget prices, but the choice is really down to personal preference. For the keyboard and mouse, stick to USB devices. When you choose a monitor, make sure you get the right cable to connect it to your PC.

The PCs we're building here have integrated Ethernet ports that you can use to connect them to a broadband router; if you'd rather connect via Wi-Fi, you'll also need to buy a USB Wi-Fi adapter. Good ones are available for less than £12 but make sure you get one that supports 802.11n Wi-Fi for the fastest possible connections.

Don't get hung up on specific model numbers

Don't worry too much about specific model numbers: the products we've chosen here don't have any magical qualities. If you're reading this book a while after it's been published, you might well find that the A75M-HVS has been replaced by the A83R-XYZ and the HyperX memory is now called the MegaX, or something along those lines. None of these things matter: what's important is that the products you choose include the features you want and get on well with the other components you're using.

For example, we've chosen the Seagate 1TB 3.5" Barracuda hard disk drive, but there's no reason why you couldn't use a completely different firm's hard disk or solid state drive instead. Provided it's the right size and uses the SATA-III standard, it will work just fine. Similarly you could happily use a different AMD processor to the one we've used in our project; as long as it's compatible with the motherboard and memory, everything will go swimmingly.

So what components did we choose? Let's have a look.

The perfect PC, mark 1

The remit for our first PC project was to build a very powerful, very expandable future-proof PC.

That made some of our decisions for us: for example, if you want maximum expandability then a full-sized ATX case is by far the best option. Having chosen a form factor, the next step was to pick a case. We went for the CM Storm Scout for several reasons: it's very big, it's very roomy, its front connectors are positioned sensibly and its integrated 700W power supply is quiet but powerful enough to drive a high-spec PC with a demanding graphics card. There's no reason why you can't buy your case and power supply separately but there was no financial benefit to us in doing so.

It's worth noting that our case comes with red LED lights that give the PC an evil glow when it's switched on. It's the sort of thing that looks quite nice in brochures but feels a bit silly in an office, so you'll be glad to know that there's a switch on the front that turns the lights off if you don't want them.

For our processor, we chose one of Intel's Core i5 processors. It isn't the fastest processor money can buy, but it isn't the best part of £1000 either and, in benchmark tests, the processor we went for (the Core i5 2500K running at 3.3GHz) delivers blistering performance. That's hardly surprising: it's a quad-core processor, which means it's exceptionally powerful. Unless you're planning to make a Pixar movie in your shed, there's no reason to choose anything more expensive. We went for Intel over AMD because, at the time of writing, Intel processors provided the best balance of performance and price for our particular project.

The Core i5 processor requires an LGA1155 socket and that – along with the ATX form factor we'd already chosen for our case – narrowed our choice of motherboards considerably. We went for an Asus board, partly because Asus has a wide range of products to fit almost any need and partly because we've used a number of Asus boards over the years and found them to be easy to install and supported with good manuals and driver discs. These things matter.

Our motherboard supports DDR3 memory, which is the latest, fastest kind of PC memory, and 8GB makes Windows really fly, especially in gaming and other demanding tasks. As with our motherboard, our choice of memory was based on prior experience and really keen prices.

It's easy to blow your budget on an expensive graphics card, but unless you're making entire animated movies or playing games on a 30" monitor there's no need to spend hundreds of pounds on a stand-alone card. We wanted a fast graphics card with 1GB of on-board memory and a decent range of connections. While some good-quality cards cost £200 upwards, our choice delivers plenty of power for half that price. The XFX HD has stacks of good reviews on the various hardware review sites, so it's a safe choice that won't break the bank.

Last but not least, there was storage to think about. In an

ideal world, we'd buy 1TB of solid-state storage but, at the time of writing, that costs over £3000 – and the same amount of storage in a traditional hard disk form will leave you change from a £50 note. Seagate's Barracuda drives are very good value for money and support the SATA-III standard, which delivers very fast performance. We also chose a Pioneer optical disc drive that reads and burns CDs and DVDs and also plays Blu-Ray movies and records on rewritable Blu-Rays for data storage. It's very unlikely that we'll see another optical disc format after Blu-Ray: movies and TV programmes are increasingly being sold as downloads rather than on discs. However, all-digital distribution is still some way off, so it's sensible to buy a drive that can cope with every current optical disc format.

Here is our shopping list:

Component	Name	Why we chose it
Case	CM Storm Scout with Coolermaster Silent Pro 700W	The Storm Scout is a solid, roomy ATX case that's very easy to set up, and the integrated power supply makes life even easier.
Power supply unit	Not required	The case we chose comes with a pre-installed power supply and it's a good one: powerful enough for hefty hardware but not so loud that your house sounds like Heathrow airport.
Processor	Intel Core i5 2500K 3.3GHz	This Intel Core i5 is a blisteringly fast but very affordable quad-core processor that can cope with the most demanding jobs.
Motherboard	Asus P8Z68-V LX	Designed for high-performance PCs, this Asus motherboard features fast USB 3.0 ports, is designed for Intel Core processors and matches our chosen processor and case.
Graphics card	XFX HD 6850 XXX Edition 1GB	A few years ago, something this powerful would have cost thousands of pounds. Based around AMD's HD 6850 graphics processor, this card has 1GB of memory and three output ports (dual DVI, HDMI and DisplayPort) for easy connection to HD TVs and high-end monitors.
Memory	Kingston HyperX DDR3 1600MHz	The more memory you have the faster your PC will go, especially with demanding tasks. We've gone for twin 4GB sticks of super-fast DDR3 RAM here so our PC really flies.
Hard disk	Seagate 1TB 3.5" Barracuda SATA-III	This isn't the fastest hard disk around but it's still pretty quick. It's one of the cheapest, reliable one-terabyte drives around.
Optical disc	Pioneer BDR-206DBK 12x BD-RE	It's a CD player, a DVD player and a Blu-Ray Disc player, and it can burn CDs, DVDs and BD-RE discs too.

PART  **The perfect PC, mark 2**

Our priorities for our second PC project were slightly
different – we wanted it to be really affordable and quiet
without skimping on performance – but as you'll see,
we've ended up with some similar components.

As with our first PC, our shopping list began with a case: we
wanted something that would fit under the TV and that looked
more like a bit of home entertainment kit than a traditional PC.
Compact cases mean compact motherboards and our chosen
case is no exception: the Antec case we liked uses a MicroATX,
not an ATX, motherboard.

If you're planning to put this kind of PC under your TV in an
entertainment unit, make sure you measure it before you buy:
cases such as this look a lot smaller in photos than they actually
are! Remember too that some cases, including this one, have their
fans at the side and not the back. You'll need to allow room for the
fans to circulate air in order to keep your PC nice and cool.

Once again our chosen case has an integrated power supply.
This time it's a 380-watt one rather than a 700-watt PSU.
That's more than enough for the things our PC will be doing
and it's been specifically designed to be as quiet as possible.
When you're building a PC to sit in the living room, every decibel
counts. It's amazing how annoying even a little bit of noise can
become when you're concentrating on the quiet bits of a film.

We're working to a tight budget here, so ideally we want
to use integrated graphics rather than a stand-alone card.
Integrated graphics had a bit of a bad name a few years ago
because they were often underpowered and, to put it politely,
rubbish. However, technology has come on in leaps and bounds
in recent years and processors such as AMD's Llano boast
very good integrated graphics: when you buy the processor,
you're effectively getting a Radeon graphics card thrown in too.
The processor we chose, the Llano A6-3500, is a triple-core
processor that runs at a nifty 2.1GHz.

Once again the processor and case dictate the motherboard:
this time we need a MicroATX model with an FM1 processor
socket. Asrock's catchily named A75M-HVS fits the bill perfectly
– and not just because it's incredibly cheap. It supports 3D
Blu-Ray discs, has integrated surround sound, makes the most
of AMD's integrated graphics technology and doesn't skimp on
connectors or expandability.

The motherboard supports DDR3 RAM, but there are only two
memory module slots. That's not a problem for us, however, as
we only need 4GB of RAM for home entertainment purposes.
The motherboard does support up to 16GB of memory, though,
so you can always replace the twin 2GB modules with twin 4GB
or even 8GB ones if you decide you need more memory in a few
years' time.

Last, but not least, we had to choose storage options – and
we went for exactly the same hard disk and optical drive as with
our first PC. That gives us plenty of storage for digital media and
an optical drive that can play everything from music CDs to Blu-
Ray movies.

Here is our shopping list:

Component	Name	Why we chose it
Case	Antec NSK 2480 MATX	This MicroATX case is designed to look like a home entertainment device and it features internal baffles that reduce the noise of key components such as the hard disk and fan.
Power supply unit	Not required	The case we chose comes with a pre-installed power supply, and it's a good one.
Processor	AMD Llano A6-3500 2.1GHz	This triple-core processor is both speedy and affordable, and will happily munch even the most demanding high-definition video clips. The Llano is based on AMD's Fusion architecture, which means it's designed to handle the graphics as well as the general processing.
Motherboard	Asrock A75M-HVS	Designed for AMD processors, the micro ATX-sized Asrock A75M-HVS has integrated high-definition graphics and surround sound and there's an integrated HDMI port for easy connection to HD TVs and screens. It's easy to expand if you want more power in the future, too.
Graphics card	Not required	Our processor has all the graphics horsepower we need. It's more than capable of delivering high-definition video to a monitor or HD TV.
Memory	Kingston HyperX DDR3 1600MHz	4GB of fast DDR3 memory is the sweet spot for this PC: we're very, very unlikely to need any more than that.
Hard disk	Seagate 1TB 3.5" Barracuda SATA-III	As with our big PC, we've gone for Seagate's bargain 1-terabyte drive here. That's stacks of room for music, photos and movies. It's quiet, too, which is handy for a PC that's likely to end up underneath the TV.
Optical disc	Pioneer BDR-206DBK 12x BD-RE	With CD, DVD and Blu-Ray support, this drive can handle any kind of media disc.

PART  # Building the perfect PC, mark 1

Now, it's time to start building your computer or, in our case, computers. In this section, we're going to build PC number one – a full-sized, quad-core, future-proof PC – and in Part 4 we'll build a more compact and slightly simpler PC that's ideal for the living room.

Building a PC doesn't take very long, but you might prefer to break the job into smaller chunks. To help with that we've divided our tutorials into sections that should make it easy to pick up from where you've left off.

PART **3** # All set?

Before you start any PC project, it's important to check that you have the right tools and the right components. Make sure you have the following:

The right components Don't assume that when you buy a component, you'll definitely receive the correct one: it's easy to click on the wrong thing when you shop online; suppliers can, and occasionally do, make mistakes. You don't want to get half way through your project and then discover that you don't have a crucial part.

The right cables Don't assume that components such as hard disks come with connecting cables: they usually don't, particularly if you've bought OEM (Original Equipment Manufacturer) versions in plain brown boxes. That's not a problem when you're building a PC from scratch, however, as your case should come with the necessary power connectors and your motherboard will include the necessary data cables. Don't start your PC project until you've located them!

The right tools A selection of Phillips and flat-head screwdrivers will make your life much easier, and a pair of long, thin, pointy-nosed pliers will be a big help when you drop a screw inside the case – which you will, because everybody does.

The right place to build it Adequate lighting is essential. Daylight is best; if that's not possible, then it's important to ensure you have appropriate task lighting. We like anglepoise lights but clip-on torches can be handy too. Your working environment should be clean, dry and dust-free.

Anti-static protection Sparks of static electricity – known in the trade as electrostatic discharge (ESD) – spell doom for computer components, so we'd advise that you invest in anti-static protection. There are two cheap and effective ways to do that: an anti-static wrist strap or an anti-static mat. In each case, you get a clip that connects the anti-static device to a suitable earthing point such as a radiator; the strap goes around your wrist and keeps you static-free, while the mat simply sits underneath the PC you're building. We prefer mats but either option will work perfectly well and keep your new PC safe from unwanted ESD.

Manuals and discs Some of your components will come with manuals and installation discs, and it's important not to lose them. Some of the manuals, such as the motherboard manual, will come in very handy when you're trying to identify tiny little cables and connectors. The discs include the necessary drivers for Windows to get the best from your hardware.

Patience Don't let a dropped screw, skipped tutorial step or forgotten cable send your blood pressure into orbit: if you stay relaxed and think logically, nothing can stop you from building the perfect PC. If at any point you get annoyed or frustrated, take a break and come back with a clear head.

An unplugged PC We can't stress this one enough. Always, and we mean always, ensure that the PC's power cable is unplugged when you're opening the case or installing components.

Let's build a PC.

PART 3 Installing the motherboard

①

Lay the case on its side, with the transparent Perspex panel facing up. We want to remove this panel so we can start installing components. Depending on the case, the panel may be secured with ordinary screws or it may be secured with thumbscrews. This case uses thumbscrews.

②

Unscrew and remove the thumbscrews and put them somewhere safe: we'll need them again when we've fitted all of the internal components. Slide the panel towards the back of the case and lift it upwards to remove it. Put the panel somewhere safe. Remove any boxes of screws and cables that you find inside the case.

③

Motherboards aren't screwed directly onto the case; they're screwed into little brass stands called stand-offs, which you'll find in one of the bags of screws that came with the case. One of the things we like about this particular case is that it comes with a little cardboard template that tells you where the standoffs should go. We're using an ATX form factor motherboard, so we need to use stand-off holes A, B, C, D, E, F, J, K and L. If your case doesn't come with similar instructions you'll need to gently insert the motherboard and work out where the stand-offs need to go by lining up its screw holes with the appropriate bits of the case.

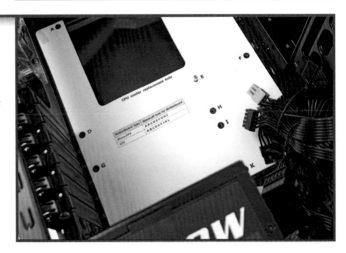

④

You don't need any tools to install the stand-offs: it's just a matter of using your fingers to turn the stand-offs until they're securely in place. Once the stand-offs are in place, remove the paper template from the case.

⑤

Stand-offs can be fiddly things but they shouldn't require any force to turn them: if a stand-off is hard to turn, it's probably crooked. Take it out and try again. If that doesn't work it might be a faulty one. Don't worry – in most cases, you'll have more stand-offs than you need. If you don't and you end up short by one stand-off, it's not the end of the world.

⑥

Your motherboard packaging will include a thin metal backing plate, which is designed to go on the back of the plate and surround the various sockets – USB ports, video outputs and so on. Line the plate up with the ports on the back of the motherboard and see if any of its pins block crucial connectors. In this case, two of the pins block one of the motherboard's video outputs, so we'll bend them back until they're out of the way. Be careful when you do this: the metal is very thin and very sharp. You wouldn't be the first person to get a nasty cut from a motherboard backing plate.

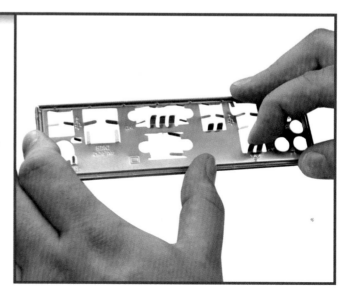

7

Check once again that the backing plate isn't going to block anything important and then gently place it in the large rectangular gap at the back of the PC case. The bent pins should be facing inwards. Make sure it's the right way up, too.

8

Carefully lift the motherboard into the case – you may have to grab a fistful of power cables to move them out of the way – and place it so its screw holes are directly above the brass stand-offs you installed a moment ago. You'll probably find that you need to fiddle with the backing plate to get it to line up perfectly. Don't worry if there appear to be more stand-offs than screw holes: while our case has nine stand-offs, our motherboard only needs six.

9

Using a Phillips screwdriver, carefully screw the motherboard into the stand-offs and stop when they become stiff. You want the screws to be tight enough that they won't move but you don't want to over-tighten them and crack the motherboard. Keep pliers handy: the screw holes near the cooling fans are very fiddly and, if you're like us, you'll probably drop the screws a couple of times. If they fall behind the motherboard and you can't reach them for love nor money, ensure the motherboard is secure, lift the PC up, turn it upside down and gently roll it around to free the missing screw. Be careful if you do this because that case is quite heavy.

Now it's time to give our PC a processor.

 PART  # Installing the processor

Once the motherboard is in place, the next step is to install the processor. It's essential that you complete every step in this section: if the processor's heatsink isn't fitted correctly or if you forget to connect its fan cable, your PC will overheat in a spectacular and expensive fashion. Nothing in this section is difficult, we promise.

The processor socket in this motherboard is protected in two ways: there's a black plastic cover over the socket itself and a locking metal cover on that. Locate the processor socket and look for the lever on the right-hand side. To unlock it, press down with your thumb or finger and pull it slightly rightwards.

Lift the lever up and push it backwards to release the metal processor cover. The cover is hinged at the back and should lift up easily now that it's been unlocked.

③

Gently remove the black plastic socket cover. You won't need this again so you can throw it away.

④

You should now see the processor socket in all its uncovered glory. We're looking for two notches, which stick out from either side of the socket at the beginning of the rear quarter of the socket. These are guides to ensure that we line up the processor correctly.

⑤

Hold the processor on either side with your fingers and with the blank metal side upwards. Don't touch the pins on the other side of the processor. Gently position the processor in the socket: if you've got it the right way round, the notches on either side of the socket should match the indentations in the processor itself. Gently drop – but don't push – the processor into place. This socket is what's known as a Zero Insertion Force (ZIF) socket, so there's no need to shove anything anywhere.

6

Close the processor socket cover – again, you shouldn't need to apply any force here – and then pull the lever forwards to lock it in place. Press down and slightly to the left to lock the lever in place. Your processor is in place. Now, we need to ensure it doesn't overheat by installing the heatsink.

7

The heatsink is a fairly hefty fan with some thermal paste underneath that, once heated, will bond it to the processor. The heatsink has four locking mechanisms, which should correspond with four holes in the motherboard. Don't apply any pressure until you're sure that the four locking mechanisms are in the correct positions.

8

With your thumb, press down on the first of the locking mechanisms to lock it into place. You'll need to use more force than you think is necessary: if it doesn't go into place with a loud, satisfying click then it isn't in properly.

9

Once you've felt the locking mechanism click into place, do the same with the other three in a diagonal pattern – so if you have done the bottom-right mechanism, do the top-left one next. If you need to remove the heatsink in future, for example because you're upgrading the processor, the locking mechanisms can be released by turning them anti-clockwise.

10

Look on the motherboard for a connector block marked CPU_FAN. This provides the power to the heatsink's fan, and you really don't want to leave this one disconnected. Uncoil the cable from the top of the fan and connect it to the CPU_FAN connector. The connector block is shaped so you can't install it the wrong way.

We have our motherboard and our processor. Next up: memory.

PART  Installing memory

Installing memory is very straightforward: all you need
to do is to ensure that you put the memory chips in the
right place and that you put them in the right way round.
In this tutorial, we install 8GB of RAM, which is more
than enough for even the most demanding applications.
Our memory is split between two memory modules with
4GB apiece, which was the most cost-effective way of
getting the capacity we needed, and our motherboard
has enough room for that with more to spare if we want
to add even more memory at a later date.

❶

*To install memory in your new PC, you need to locate the
appropriate sockets. If your motherboard has room for four
memory modules, they'll be organised as two pairs: two primary
sockets and two secondary ones. If you only have two memory
modules – like we have – then the primary ones are the ones
you want. To make things easier for us, the motherboard
manufacturer has made the primary sockets blue so they're easy
to spot. If yours hasn't done that, check the manual to identify
which sockets are the primary ones.*

❷

*Memory modules are secured in place with little plastic clips and
you'll need to open them before you can install your RAM. To
open the clip, just press down on it with the tip of a finger. Do
the same for the clip on the other side of the socket.*

3

Memory modules and sockets are shaped in such a way that you can't install modules the wrong way around, and there's an off-centre notch that breaks each socket into two sections. Without using any pressure, line up the memory module so that the notch corresponds to the gap in the module's pins.

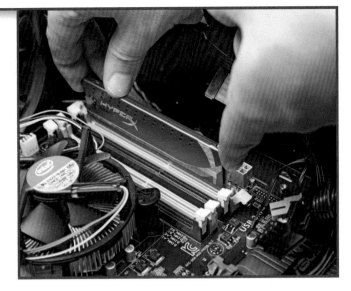

4

When you're sure that the memory module is lined up correctly, push down on both sides until the locks at the side of the socket click into place. If the memory module is fully inserted, the locks should do their job automatically. It's very like installing the processor heatsink: the amount of pressure you need to exert is just enough to make you a bit worried.

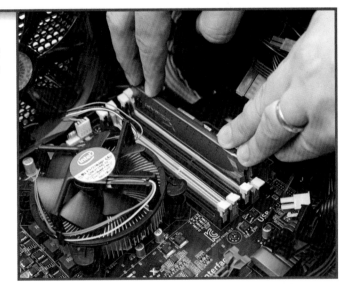

5

Repeat the process for the second memory module, if you have one. Remember to use the remaining primary memory slot, which is coloured blue on this motherboard.

There's only one more thing we need to add to the motherboard: the graphics card.

PART ③ Installing the graphics card

Not everybody needs a dedicated graphics card. If you've decided to stick with the motherboard's integrated graphics technology, which is fine for everyday computer use, then you can skip this step. If you want to get the best out of games or graphics-intensive work, such as image editing or video editing, however, then a discrete graphics card is still a must-have purchase.

①

The first step here is to work out where the graphics card will go. Our card is a PCI Express card, which means it'll slot into the large, dark blue slot you can see in the middle of the picture (the one immediately above the text 'Windows 7 Ready'). The card is more than one slot wide, so it'll also sit on top of the little dark blue slot above the PCI Express slot.

②

Now we've located the graphics card slot, we need to remove the backing plates from the case so that the card's connections can be accessed from the back of our PC. Before you can remove them you need to loosen them; how you do that depends on the kind of case you have: on some cases the backing plates are secured with screws but on ours they're held in place with springy bits of metal.

3

In our case we need to unlock the plates by pressing down on the centre of the securing prongs; if your case plates are secured with screws then of course you'll need to unscrew them. Our graphics card has two lots of connectors and takes two cards' worth of room, so we need to remove two backing plates.

4

Installing the graphics card is very like installing a memory module: line up the connector pins and when you're sure it's in the right place, push down hard to install it.

5

You don't want the graphics card to wiggle around when you connect external cables, as that could damage the card or crack your motherboard. Use the supplied screws to secure the graphics card to the back of your PC case.

6

Modern graphics cards can be hungry beasts, and our card needs its own cable running from the power supply. The connector we're looking for is a six-pin PCI power connector, which looks like this. The grey end will go into the back of the power supply and the black end will go into our graphics card. This particular cable can also be used for eight-pin PCI connections, although we don't need those extra pins here.

7

Look at the case's power supply – you may need to move some cables out of the way to do this – and identify the six-pin PCI power connectors, which are the grey sockets you can see in the centre of the photograph.

8

The connectors and sockets are shaped in such a way that you can't connect them the wrong way around by accident. Press the grey end of the cable into the appropriate socket.

9

As you've probably guessed, the next step is to connect the other end of the power cable to the graphics card. The particular case, motherboard and graphics card combination we've chosen means that there isn't a great deal of room to do this, so this step is a little bit fiddly.

The graphics card is the last component we're installing directly onto the motherboard, so let's start cabling everything up.

PART  **Connecting the cables**

We've got good news and bad news for you. The good news is that all of the cables you'll need for this section should have come with your PC case and motherboard, and they'll usually be labelled for easy identification. The bad news is that some of the cables you'll need won't seem long enough, and you'll need to do some crafty re-routing to make everything stretch. Once again nothing here is difficult, although a couple of the steps are quite annoying. Sorry!

The first connector we need to identify is the main 24-pin power connector for the motherboard, which is a great big block with multi-coloured wires going into it. The socket for this connector is just above and to the right of our motherboard's memory modules. Locate the connector and the socket and put the former into the latter.

Now, we need to connect a second power block. This one's an eight-pin connector with black and yellow wires; it goes into the socket marked EATX12V. On our motherboard, this socket is towards the top-left corner, above and to the left of the processor and heatsink.

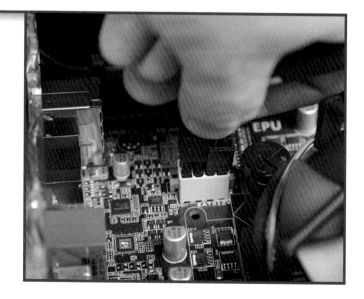

3

The case will also have some connectors marked USB; as you might expect, they connect to the USB sockets on the motherboard: on our motherboard those sockets are right at the bottom. Once again, the connectors are shaped so that they can't be installed incorrectly.

4

The candy-coloured cables you see here are for the front panel connectors: the reset button, the power button and the system speaker. These connectors are very small and fiddly, and you'll need to refer to your motherboard's manual for the precise layout.

5

Our motherboard and case also support an external SATA, a connector that enables you to use very fast external hard disks. The cable for this one is red and connects to one of the connectors marked SATA 6Gb/s on the motherboard, just above and to the right of the USB connectors.

6

Houston, we have a problem: we need to connect the HD audio connector to the appropriate part of the motherboard, but the cable simply doesn't reach. It is actually long enough – it's just in the wrong place. To get at it, we need to put the PC upright and remove the other side panel so that we can access it.

7

If you were to give the HD audio cable a good tug, it would barely move. That's because it's secured to a bunch of other cables with a black plastic cable tie. Using pliers or a pair of scissors, very carefully cut the cable tie to free up the HD audio cable.

8

If you've got one handy – our case came with a few spares – use a fresh cable tie to keep the remaining cables together, making sure you don't include the HD audio cable when you do. Don't worry if you don't have spare cable ties; this step is just for neatness rather than for any particular technological reason.

9

Don't refit the side panel just yet – we'll need to get in there again later – but lie your PC down again with the open side facing upwards. You should now be able to get the extra couple of centimetres necessary to make the HD audio cable reach the audio socket on the back of the motherboard.

We're nearly finished. All that's left to do now is install the hard disk and optical drive, and we've built an entire PC.

PART  Installing the hard disk and optical drive

We're on the home stretch now: the motherboard's in place, we've installed the memory and graphics cards and we've connected all of the crucial components together. The only components we've still to add are our disk drives: a hard disk and a Blu-Ray/DVD/CD player. The case we've chosen makes these steps particularly easy.

Before we install the drives we need to locate the correct cables. We need two SATA data cables (which are the ones with the black and white connectors on the left of the photograph) and we also need a long SATA power cable. That's the black cable with the multiple connectors (on the right). The SATA data cables should have come with your motherboard, while the power cable should have come with your PC case.

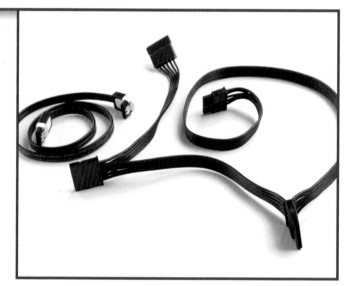

Connect the SATA power supply to the back of the case's power supply – once again it's shaped so you can't put it in the wrong way – and run the cable into the empty drive bays at the front of the case. That is where we're going to put the hard disk drive and the optical drive.

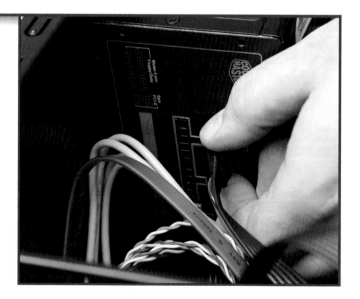

3

We've got two identical SATA cables to connect, but we're not going to connect them in identical ways. Our motherboard has two kinds of SATA data connectors: high-speed 6Gbps ones and slightly slower 3Gbps ones. Our hard disk can use 6Gbps speeds but our optical drive can't, so connect one of the SATA data cables to a 6Gbps socket (it'll be marked SATA6G) and the other to a 3Gbps one (marked SATA3G).

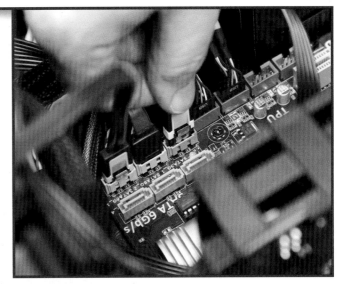

4

Feed the 6Gbps SATA data cable into the same space that you ran the SATA power cable and put the 3Gbps one towards the top of the PC's case (if you're looking at the case from the front, the top is to the right as the PC's still on its side).

5

While many cases use good old-fashioned screws to install hard disks, our case has a more elegant option: it comes with a collection of clips that pop into the screw holes on the hard disk and lock the drive into place without turning a single screw. You'll need two. The L-shaped ends go at the opposite end from the hard disk's data and power connectors.

6

Holding the clips in place with your left hand – they'll fall off if you don't – connect the SATA data cable and power cables, ensuring that when you connect the power you use the middle connector block: the cable has to run to the top of the case and power the optical drive too.

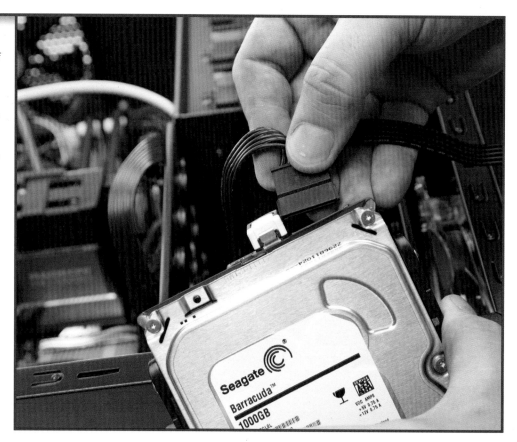

7

Slide the hard disk into the first available slot in the hard disk cage. While there are several slots to choose from here, the power cable isn't very long: the nearer to the top you place the hard disk, the happier the next few steps will be. Push the hard disk until it clicks into place; if you need to get it out again, you can unclip it by pressing the ends of the clips and pulling the hard disk towards you.

8

Hard disks don't need to be accessible from outside, but optical ones do, otherwise you won't be able to put CD, DVD or Blu-Ray discs in them. That means we need to take off the front of our case. To do this, grab the bottom of the case front and pull it towards you.

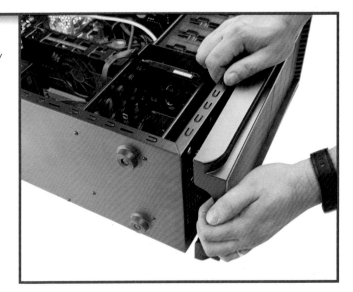

9

The case front has blanking plates, which are designed so that there aren't any big holes in the case when there don't need to be. The plates are held in place with a plastic clip on either side. Unclip the top one and remove it, but leave the others where they are.

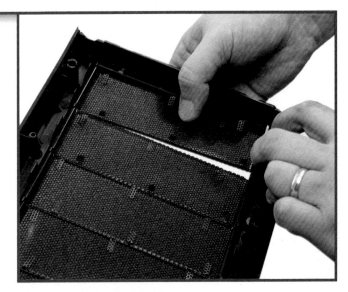

10

Once again, the case manufacturer has decided against screws: the optical drive will be secured by a quick-release locking mechanism. Before you insert the drive, make sure the top mechanism is unlocked by pushing the lock backwards and upwards. Once you've done that, make sure you've got the drive the correct way up – the top should be towards the top of the case, on your right – and push it into place. The drive will stick out a few centimetres from the case as it needs to sit flush with the case cover.

Locking the drive in place is simple: slide the lock towards you and then down until it locks with a click. Give the drive a gentle tug to make sure it won't move when you press its eject button or insert a disk.

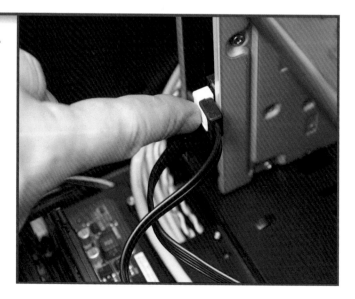

Locate the SATA power connector that's already hooked up to the hard disk and connect it to the appropriate slot on the back of the optical drive. There isn't an awful lot of cable to play with here so this step is a bit fiddly; if the cable just won't reach then you might want to remove the optical drive, put it in a lower drive bay and then connect it.

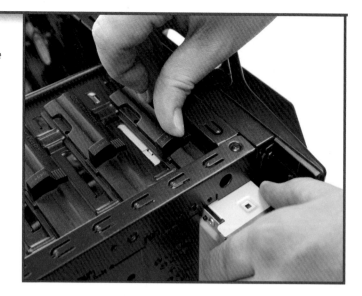

Locate the SATA data connector and push it into the appropriate slot in the back of the optical drive. As with the power connector, it's shaped in such a way that you can't connect it incorrectly.

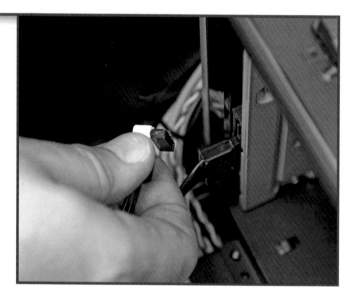

We don't need to get into the optical drive any more so it's time to replace the front of the PC case. If everything's gone smoothly, the front of the optical drive should fit into the space you made and should be flush with the front panel.

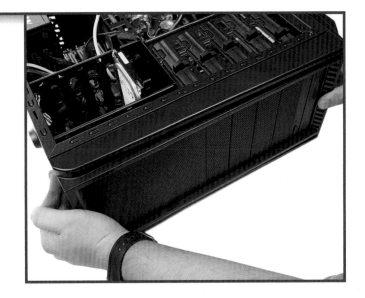

There's only one step to go: we need to provide power to the case's various fans. The cable for this should have been supplied with the case and will have several rectangular four-pin power connectors on it. These connect to the rectangular white power connectors for the case fans. In our case, there are three, one of which is hiding behind the other side panel of the PC. Aren't you glad we didn't refit that panel earlier? Make sure you connect all of the fans: they're there for a reason.

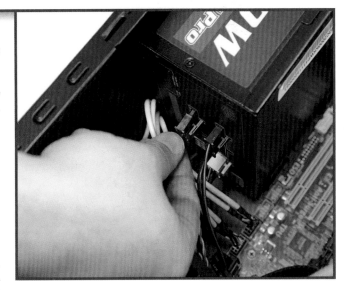

Refit the two side panels and make sure they're flush with the front panel. Secure the panels in place with the thumbscrews you removed earlier, connect your keyboard, monitor and mouse, connect the power cable and plug the other end into a wall socket. Your new PC is ready to run for the very first time.

4

PART 4 Building the perfect PC, mark 2

In this tutorial, we build our second PC, which is designed to be a living room PC. It's perfectly capable of all kinds of tasks but, as we don't need it to be ridiculously, blisteringly quick, we don't need quite as many components. The good news is that this PC is a bit simpler and easier to build than our first PC – but the bad news is that the more compact case means that a few bits are quite fiddly.

PART 4 Installing the processor and memory

In our first project, we put the motherboard into the case before adding key components such as the processor and memory modules, but this PC's more compact case gives us less room to manoeuvre. As a result we'll do things slightly differently this time: we'll install the processor and RAM before we put the motherboard into the case.

1

Remove the motherboard from its packaging, put the included SATA data cables to one side and keep the motherboard on its squishy foam protector: this enables you to install the next few components without scratching your worktop or table and without damaging your motherboard. If your chosen motherboard didn't come with any foam, improvise: just make sure that whatever you choose isn't full of static. As with our previous project, an anti-static mat or wrist band is strongly recommended.

2

The processor socket is locked in place with a thin metal lever. In our photograph, it's located at the top end of the processor socket. To unclip it, push it down and move it slightly away from the processor socket.

3

Lift the lever upwards and away from the processor socket to fully unlock it. Now, examine the socket closely: one of the corners will have a triangular section removed. This is to help you put the processor in the correct way round.

4

Take the processor out of its packaging, holding it by the edges with the smooth metal side up to ensure that you don't touch the pins. If you examine it closely you'll see that one of the corners has a triangle printed on it. This, as you've probably guessed, is the corner that matches up with the shaped bit of the processor socket.

5

Holding the processor by its edges – you should never touch the pins – you can now lower it gently into the processor socket. As with our earlier PC, this is a Zero Insertion Force (ZIF) socket: if the processor is lined up correctly it should drop into place without any effort whatsoever. If it's not quite right, just lift it up and gently try again until it pops into place. Never, ever try to force a processor into a socket. That just damages it.

6

The processor socket on this motherboard doesn't have a cover, but don't worry: it'll still keep the CPU in its right place. To lock the processor to the motherboard, pull the locking lever forwards and tuck it in place by pushing it down and towards the socket until it's secure. Your processor is now bonded solidly to the motherboard. If you want to remove it in the future, you need to remove the heatsink – more of that in a moment – and unlock the processor socket lever so that you can lift the processor out.

7

Now it's time to install the heatsink. Lift the heatsink out of its packaging with the fan side up and don't touch the other side: that's covered with a special thermal paste that bonds to the top of the processor and you don't want any dust or oil to compromise it. Unlike Intel heatsinks, which attach to the motherboard with four locking mechanisms, AMD ones use two: a metal clip on one side and a metal one with a plastic lock on the other.

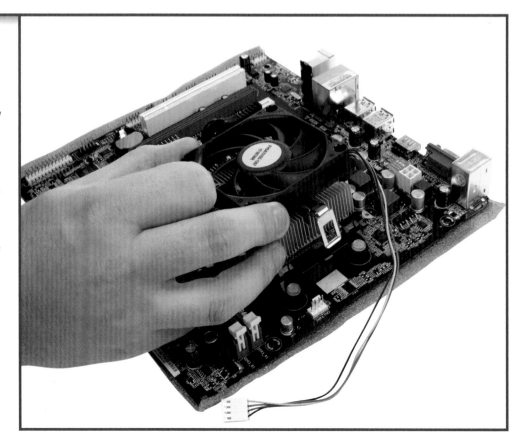

8

Unwind the fan connector cable from the top of the heat sink and position the heatsink so that its clips line up with, and sit over, the appropriate plastic nubs on either side of the processor socket. In our photo, the metal clip goes on the right-hand side and the locking clip goes on the left-hand side.

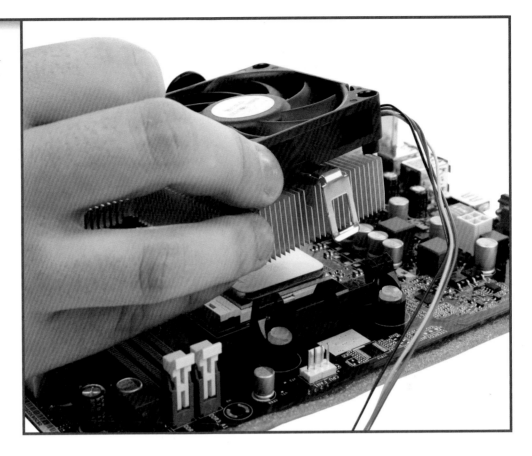

9

Once you're confident that the heatsink clips are lined up correctly, press the metal one down to secure it to the plastic nub. If the heatsink isn't perfectly positioned, you won't be able to close the clip: if that's the case, lift the heatsink up again and gently reposition it.

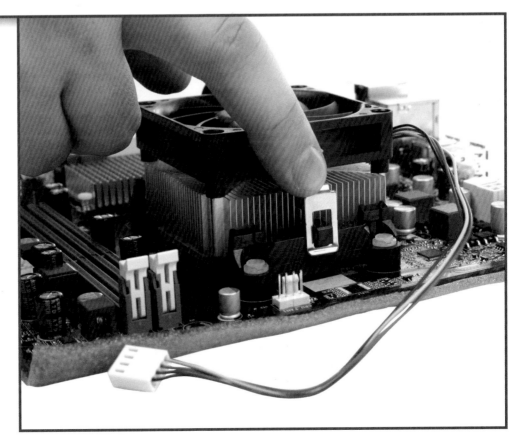

The locking clip looks complicated, but don't worry: it isn't! Make sure that the metal part of the clip is correctly positioned over the plastic nub and then push the plastic lever clockwise to lock the clip – and the heatsink – into place.

Securing the plastic lock is one of those jobs that requires a surprising amount of pressure but, as long as the clips are in the right place and the bottom of your motherboard is adequately cushioned, there's no risk of damaging anything. If you want to remove the heatsink in the future, for example because you want to install a more powerful processor, removal is just a matter of unlocking the clips and twisting the heatsink to break the join between it and the processor.

The heatsink does its best to dissipate heat from the processor, but it needs a fan to help: without it, your PC won't last for very long before it overheats. Locate the CPU_FAN1 connector on the motherboard – on ours, it's placed nice and close to the processor socket – and connect the heatsink's fan cable to it.

We've given our PC a processor; now, let's give it some memory. Our motherboard has two memory module slots and they're easy to spot because they're the biggest things on the board and they're coloured a nice bright blue. Each slot has a retaining clip on each side. Open the clips by pressing on them with your finger. As we're installing two memory modules, we'll need to open all four clips on the two slots.

The connecting pins on the bottom of the memory module are split into two unequally-sized sections and you'll see that the memory module slot is similarly shaped: this is to ensure that you can only install the memory modules the correct way round. Make sure the modules are lined up correctly with the slots and then press down on the two corners until the locking clips click into place.

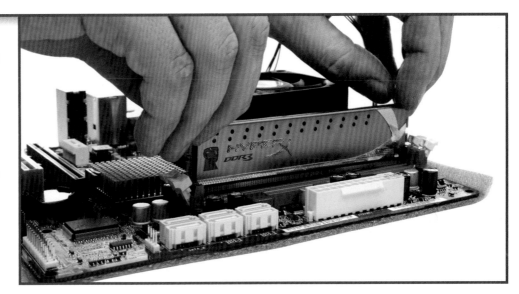

If, like us, you're installing two memory modules, repeat the process with the second module. When both modules are installed, the end result should look something like this. If the clips aren't fully locked in place that means the modules aren't fully inserted.

This PC doesn't need an external graphics card, so we're ready to put the motherboard into the case.

PART 4 Installing the motherboard

With a compact case, it's much easier to fit the major components when the motherboard isn't already installed in the case, but for everything else the motherboard needs to be fitted before we can continue. While every case is slightly different, the basic process is the same: you need to ensure that the motherboard is screwed securely in place. To do that you need to screw the motherboard

onto stand-offs, which are little brass sockets that are screwed into the PC case. If the stand-offs are already pre-installed, which they are with some cases, then you might have to move them to match the holes in your chosen motherboard. Whatever you do, don't try to force your motherboard into position: doing that might crack it and such cracks can be fatal to delicate electronics.

The case we've chosen for this PC looks very different to the one in our first project: it's designed to look good in a living room, so it's been styled to resemble other consumer electronics, such as DVD players and hi-fi equipment. It's bigger than it looks, however, so make sure there's enough room under your TV (or wherever you want to put it) when you're ordering the case and allow room for cooling, too. The circles you can see on the right hand side of the case are cooling fans and they need space to do their job. If they're blocked, your PC could overheat.

Like most modern PC cases, ours uses a thumbscrew to hold the removable panels in place: in this case the thumbscrew's located in the middle of the panel at the top of the case. Unscrew the thumbscrew and put it somewhere safe: you'll need it to close the case again when you've built your PC.

3

Lift off the top panel of the case and you should see something like this. Our case is quite unusual, as it's been designed to operate as quietly as possible: that means there are lots of internal dividers, as well as noise-reducing ideas such as rubber stoppers to prevent vibrations from the optical drive from resonating. Remove the supplied bag of screws and additional plastic dividers before proceeding.

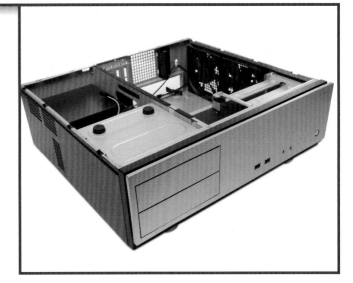

4

Unlike the case we used in our first PC project, this one doesn't come with a paper template showing where the stand-offs go – so we'll need to work that out for ourselves. Gently lift the motherboard into position inside the case and line up its screw holes with the holes in the PC casing. You'll need good lighting for this, so a little LED torch might come in handy here. Make sure that when you do this, the motherboard is positioned flush to the back of the case: the case provides more space than the motherboard actually needs.

5

You'll find a bunch of stand-offs in the bag of screws that came with the case. Using your fingers, screw the stand-offs into the case at the points where you'll screw in the motherboard. Don't worry if you end up with spare ones: most cases come with more stand-offs than you actually need, because they're fiddly things and easy to lose. If the stand-off feels difficult to tighten, check it's in at the right angle; if it is, you might have a duff one, so grab another and use it instead.

Locate the thin metal
backplate that came with your
motherboard and hold it over
the motherboard's various
connectors (video, HDMI, sound
and so on) to see if any of the
metal pins would block any of
the ports. If some do, turn the
plate over and carefully bend the
pins towards you until they're
at 90 degrees to the rest of the
plate. Be very careful when you
do this, as the backing plate is
razor-thin and razor-sharp too.
A cut won't hurt much but we
know from bitter experience that
it can make a spectacular mess!

Make sure the backplate is the
right way up and that any bent
pins are facing inwards, then
place it in the slot at the back
of the case. You might need to
move some cables out of the
way to do this and, depending
on the case, that might involve
cutting a few cable ties so
there's sufficient room to
move. The trick is to keep the
backplate in place as you put
the motherboard into the case:
if it keeps falling backwards,
raise the opposite corner of
the case slightly.

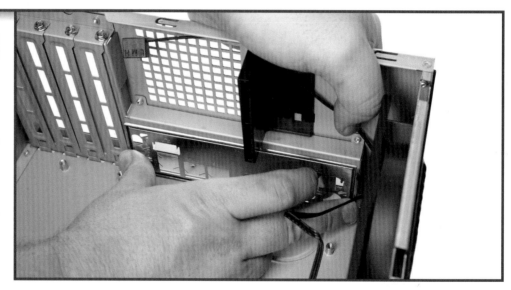

As we mentioned earlier, the
case is slightly bigger than
our motherboard. That's not
a problem: just make sure
that the motherboard is tight
against the rear of the case
and that the various monitor,
sound and USB connectors
are flush with the backplate.
If they aren't, it'll be hard
to connect or disconnect
anything.

9

Screw the motherboard onto the stand-offs you fitted earlier. Keep turning until the screws are tight, but don't over-tighten them: motherboards are fragile things and cracks can render them useless. If you drop a screw, lift the case slightly and it should roll into the space you can see to the right of the motherboard.

10

The next step is to connect the case fans to the motherboard. Our case has two fans, so we need to connect two fan cables. The cables should be easy to identify: in this case they're black with rectangular connectors on the end. Connect the first cable to the PWR_FAN1 socket on the motherboard.

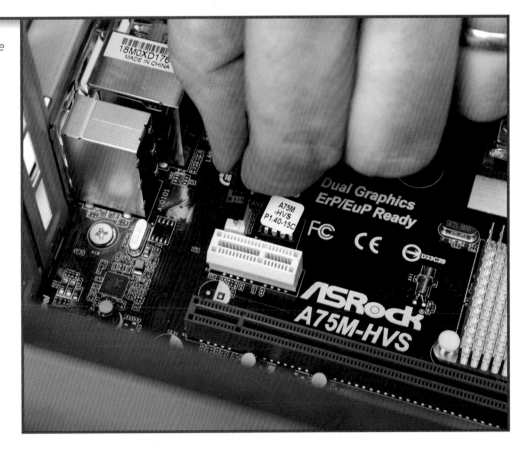

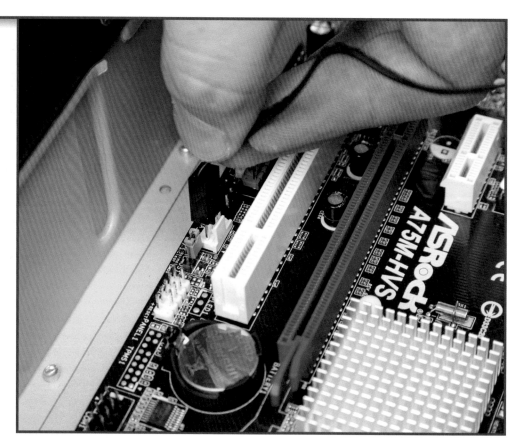

The connectors are shaped so that you can't hook them up the wrong way around. Once you've connected the first fan to PWR_FAN1, connect the second one to CHA_FAN1. This connector has four pins, not three, but once again it's shaped in such a way that you can't connect it the wrong way around.

You'll need the motherboard manual for this step. We need to connect the front panel connectors for the power button and reset button. Locate the connectors on the motherboard – in this photo they're just to the left of the fan connector we used in Step 11 – and then use the diagram in the motherboard manual (it's on page 22 in our manual) to see which connector goes where. With the exception of LEDs, it doesn't really matter whether the connectors are back to front or not; with LEDs, though, if it's connected backwards the light on the front of the panel will either not light at all or will stay lit all the time. It's easy enough to fix: just unplug it from the motherboard, turn the connector the other way round and plug it back in again.

Now, let's connect some of
the other front ports to the
motherboard. First up, the
USB slots. Locate the cable
marked USB and insert it into
the motherboard connector
marked USB 6_7, which is
to the right of the front panel
switch connectors we used in
Step 12. The USB connector
is shaped and will only go in
one way.

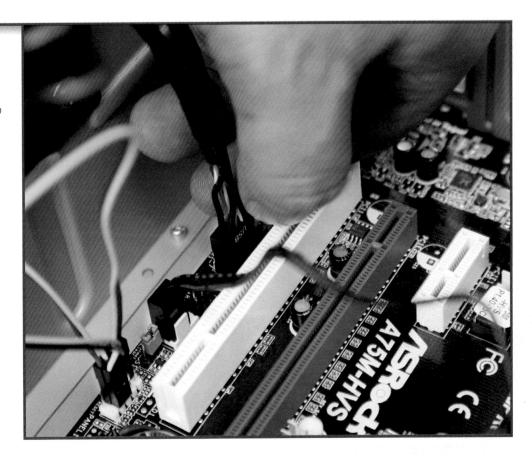

Staying in the same corner
of the motherboard, locate
the HD_AUDIO1 socket and
plug the cable marked HD
Audio into it. Once again, it's
a shaped connector that can
only be connected one way.

We're nearly finished: we've
installed the processor
and memory, installed the
motherboard and connected
it to the case fans and front
panel switches and ports.
All that's left to do now is
to install the hard disk and
optical disc drive.

PART 4 Installing the hard disk and optical drive

We're going to install two kinds of drive: a hard disk for storage and an optical disc drive that can read CDs, DVDs and Blu-Ray discs and can also burn CDs and DVDs. If you want your PC to be even quieter, you could always go for a solid-state drive instead of a traditional hard disk but at the time of writing the difference in price between hard disks and solid state disks is enormous, so we're sticking with tradition here.

1

In this case, the hard disk is held in place by a metal bracket. To fit it, we need to get the bracket out. It's held in place with four Phillips screws: unscrew them and keep them somewhere safe. You can now remove the bracket. Turn the PC on its side, with the front panel facing down. Make sure it's sitting on something soft to prevent scratching it or your worktop.

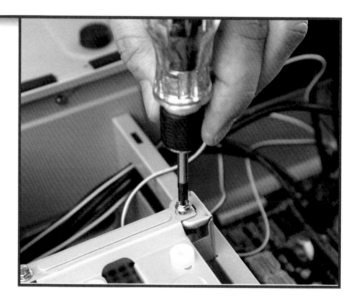

2

The hard disk goes immediately underneath the fans, as shown in our picture: it should be positioned with the screw holes facing you, the connectors facing left and the label facing upwards. The next bit's a little bit tricky: you need to hold the hard disk where it is while screwing in screws from the other side of the case.

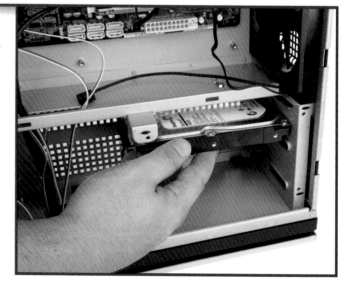

3

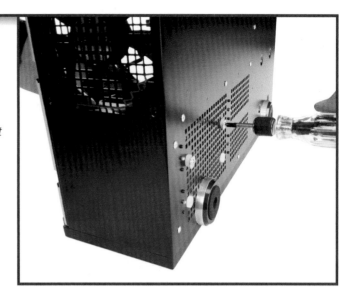

On the bottom of the case – which is currently vertical – you'll see four screw holes with plastic washers on them. The ones we want are the two at the top: we need to use them to screw the hard disk into place. The plastic is there to prevent vibration from the disk resonating throughout the case. Once you've finished with both screws – stop when they're tight, rather than trying to make them flush with the plastic; they're designed to sit proud of the washers – put the case back on its feet again.

4

Remember the bracket you took out in Step 1? It's time to put it back again. Ensuring that the hard disk is still sitting happily vertical, place the bracket over it and secure the bracket at all four corners using the screws you removed previously. Once you've done that, take two screws and screw them into the hard disk through the white plastic washers. As before, stop when they feel tight: they'll sit slightly proud of the washers.

5

Take one of the SATA data cables that came with your motherboard and connect it to the appropriate slot in the back of the hard disk. The connectors are L-shaped and can't be connected the wrong way.

Feed the cable through the hole in the panel that separates the hard disk enclosure from the motherboard and connect it to SATA_1 on the motherboard. Once again the connector is shaped for easy connection.

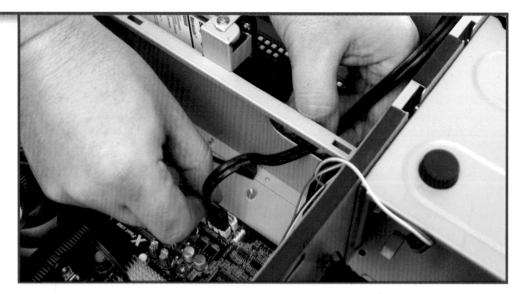

Now, we want to install our optical drive. It is designed to sit in a removable cage, known as a caddy, which sits at the front of the case behind the front panel. The caddy isn't screwed in place: remove it by lifting it up from the rear, as shown in our photo, and lifting it out of the case.

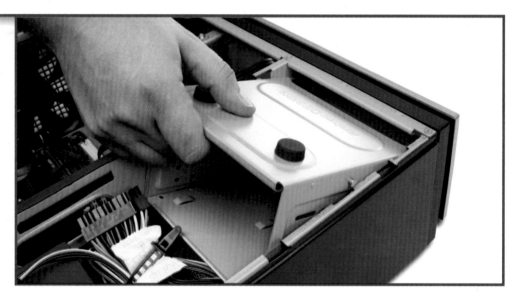

We'll need to be able to get discs in and out of the drive, so we need to remove one of the two cover plates on the case's front panel. The plates are made of plastic, are secured with little clips and can be removed by giving them a decent push. Remove the top plate but leave the bottom one where it is.

9

Now, we need to fix the optical disc drive in the drive caddy. To do this, place it at the top of the caddy – the top is the bit with the rubber pads on it – and screw it into place with two screws on each side. Use the small round screw holes rather than the elongated ones. The drive will stick out a bit from the front and that's deliberate: it needs to be flush with the front panel of the case, so it needs those extra few centimetres.

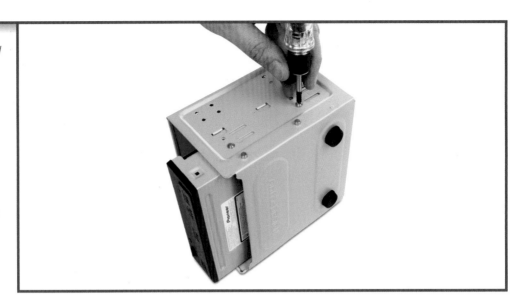

10

Put the drive caddy aside for a moment and turn your attention to the clump of cables attached to the case's power supply unit, which is the big black box at the rear left of the case. Unclip the cable tie that keeps all of the power cables together.

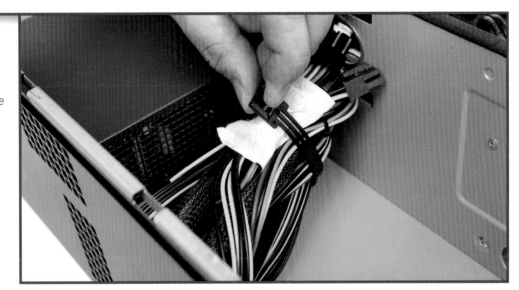

11

Before we can continue, we need to remove the black plastic baffle that separates the power supply unit's chamber from the rest of the case. It's held in place with a single screw: unscrew it, remove it and put it and the baffle somewhere safe.

12

Removing the baffle gives you a decent-sized gap that you can now feed the various power cables through. We want the two motherboard power connectors, which have rectangular eight-pin and 24-pin connector blocks.

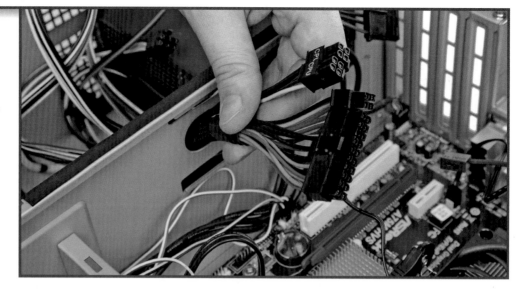

13

The first thing we want to locate is the eight-pin power connector, which our motherboard manufacturer has very helpfully labelled with a bright pink sticker.

14

Remove the sticker and connect the eight-pin connector block. The pins are shaped so that they can't be put in incorrectly.

Now, we need to repeat the process for the 24-pin power connector. Once again, our motherboard manufacturer has provided us with a cheery label, this time in bright yellow.

Once you've located the socket, remove the sticker and connect the 24-pin power block. Once again, it's shaped so that you can't connect it the wrong way round.

Now, we want to run some power to our hard disk and optical drives. The cable we want is the multicoloured SATA power cable, which has one rectangular Molex power connector and two SATA power connectors on it. Run this cable into the drive enclosure via the hole in the case and connect it to the SATA power connector on the back of your hard disk. Use the connector in the middle of the cable, not the one on the end: we need it for the optical disc drive.

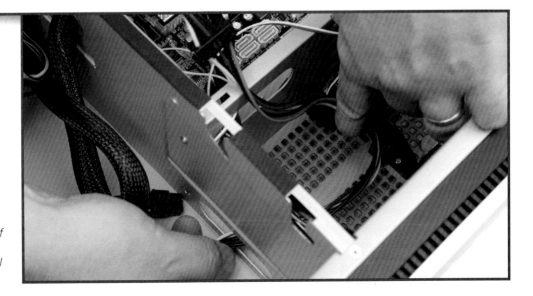

18

Now, we need to connect the power buttons for the front of the case. The power cable we're looking for is a four-pin Molex connector, which is shaped for easy connection.

19

Now, we'll take the second SATA data cable that came with our motherboard and connect it to a free SATA socket on the motherboard. Route the cable through the hole in the case divider and leave it close to where the optical disc drive will go.

20

Before we make the final connections we need to make sure that the optical disc drive is in the right place. To do this, lower the drive caddy into place. You'll need to do this at a slight angle and then push the caddy forward so that the front of the drive sits in the gap in the front of the case.

The front of the optical drive should be flush with the front panel of the PC case. If it isn't, take the caddy out again and try different screw holes to reposition the disc drive.

Lift up the back of the caddy so that you can access the connectors on the back of the optical drive. Connect one of the SATA data cables and then connect the SATA power cable. There's very little room for manoeuvre here: the cable has very little give in it, so this step can be very fiddly. If the cable won't stretch, lower the caddy a bit so it doesn't have so far to travel.

Lower the caddy into place and push it forward again. Refit the plastic baffle between the power supply chamber and the rest of the case. You can now put the top of the case back on. Secure the case top with the thumbscrew you removed earlier, connect your keyboard, monitor and mouse, connect the power cable and plug the other end into a wall socket. Your new PC is ready to run for the very first time.

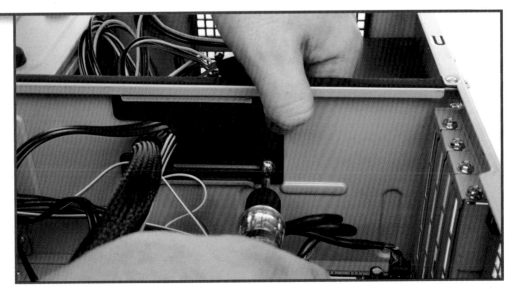

PART **5** **Final touches**

We told you building a PC was easy: now all that's left
to do is to check that everything's working okay and to
install Windows. In this section, we'll also discover some
of the best, free software that you can download and
install on your PC.

PART 5

Connecting a monitor and switching on

At this point in the proceedings, you might be tempted to rush into further installations: a sound card, perhaps, or an internal modem or network card. However, now is the time to establish that everything has gone according to plan so far. Adding extra components merely complicates troubleshooting, should any be required.

With a monitor and keyboard connected, and optionally a mouse, give your new computer its first trial run.

Check it out

Give your work-in-progress a thorough once-over. Check that the heatsink and case fans are all still connected to the motherboard, that the memory modules are still clipped into their DIMMs, that the drives are all wired-up with ribbon and power cables, and that the video card is fully secured in its slot. You might like to reassemble the case now but it's not strictly necessary. You can even leave the case lying on its side to better monitor the action. However ... you will be working with live electricity from here on so never touch anything inside your PC's case while the PSU is connected to the mains power. Even when you turn off your computer, the PSU continues to draw power from the mains and the motherboard remains in a partially-powered standby state. We're only talking a 5V current, to be fair, but it's simply crazy to work on a 'live' motherboard or anything connected to it.

True, you could flip the PSU to Off (if it has its own power switch) and/or turn off the electricity at the wall socket (and hope that Junior doesn't turn it back on for a laugh while your head is buried in the case), but it's better and safer to get into the habit of always removing the power cable before conducting any internal work. This is the only cast-iron way to ensure no physical connection between yourself and the National Grid.

Booting up ... and down again

Connect the monitor to the video card's VGA, DVI or HDMI port and plug it in to the mains. Turn on the monitor now. You might see a 'no signal' or similar message on the screen.

Now check that the PSU is set to the correct voltage – 220/230V in the UK – and connect it to the mains with your second power cable. Flip the PSU's power switch to the on position. Finally, press the on/off button on the front of the case. Your PC will come to life for the first time.

Look inside the case and check – by observation, not by touch – that the case fans are whirring. Don't worry if the heatsink fan isn't moving: modern processors and motherboards turn the heatsink fan on and off as required, so the heatsink might not need cooling when you first switch it on. If the case fan isn't working, however, kill the power immediately and check all the fan connections on the motherboard.

All being well, power your computer down with the on/off button and unplug the power cable. Leave the power switch on the PSU at the on position from now on. If all is not well, skip to p.146 now for some troubleshooting procedures.

Let us now turn our attention to some important configuration settings.

Once you're sure all your components are connected, you can put your PC's case back together.

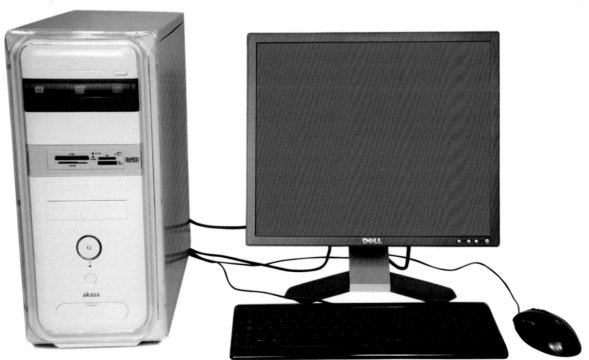

PART Essential system settings

The hard work is over, and you're nearly ready to use your brand new PC. However, before you can do that you need to know about two acronyms: POST and BIOS. POST stands for Power On Self Test and it tells you whether your PC is working properly. BIOS, pronounced 'bye-oss', is short for Basic Input and Output System and it tells your PC what bits are inside it and what to do with them.

When you switch on your PC, however, you might encounter a very small but very annoying problem: your keyboard isn't working. While modern motherboards come stuffed with USB ports and support USB keyboards, it's not unheard of for USB keyboard support to be turned off by default. If that's the case you'll need to go into the system BIOS and enable keyboard support – and to do that, you'll need a keyboard.

There are two solutions. You can beg or borrow an old, non-USB keyboard, or you can use a USB to PS/2 adapter. Whichever option you use, you can switch on your motherboard's USB keyboard support and then get rid of the old keyboard or the adapter.

Our photo shows a standard USB to PS/2 adapter, which fits

If your motherboard's USB support is turned off by default, you'll need one of these: it's a PS2 adapter that persuades your PC you have an old-style keyboard.

over the USB socket on your keyboard cable and enables you to plug it into the old-style PS/2 port on the back of the PC. If you're lucky, your USB keyboard will have come with such an adapter and you'll still have it; however if you're like us, you threw it out years ago. That means you'll have to nip to the supermarket to buy an ultra-cheap keyboard that includes the appropriate adapter.

Once you've installed the adapter or connected an old keyboard, it's time to switch on your PC and see what the POST has to say.

Beep codes

When you switch on your PC, you should hear a beep. What

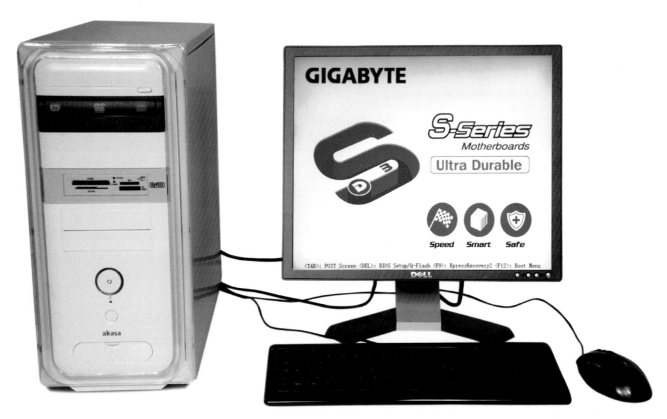

When you switch on your PC, you should see the splash screen. This is mainly an advert for the motherboard manufacturer, but it also tells you what keys to press if you want to access the BIOS setup.

you're hearing is the result of the Power On Self Test, and if you have any major hardware problem you'll find out about it now. One beep is good, because it means that the POST hasn't found any problems. More than one beep isn't so good, because it means POST has found something bad.

The beep codes you hear will depend on which company created the BIOS, and you'll see their name on the screen that appears when you first power up your PC (provided, of course, that your video card is working). For example, if your motherboard uses a Phoenix BIOS and you hear one beep, then four beeps, then two beeps, POST is telling you that your memory isn't working; if you can't see anything on screen and you hear three beeps, then another three beeps, then four beeps, the motherboard can't find your video card. That might mean it isn't installed correctly or it could indicate that the video card is faulty. For advice on troubleshooting your PC, turn to p.146; for a full list of beep codes, turn to Appendix 3.

In most cases you'll hear a single, happy beep and the screen will display the 'splash page' that appears when you first boot your PC. This screen will tell you what key you need to press to enter the BIOS settings; we need to press <DEL> for the Asus motherboard (PC mark 1) and <F2> for the Asrock motherboard (PC mark 2) while the splash screen is displayed. If you don't press the appropriate key in time, don't worry; just reboot your PC and try again. After a few moments you should see your PC's BIOS and, while it looks quite scary, it's actually rather simple.

Changing BIOS settings

You can enter your PC's BIOS by pressing the appropriate key when the first boot screen appears. In the case of our ASUS motherboard, we need to press the <DEL> key. If we don't, the PC will attempt to boot into its operating system.

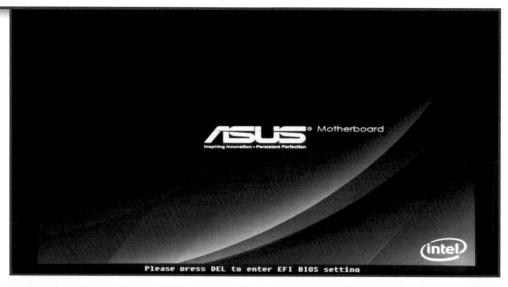

BIOS screens used to be simple text-only affairs, but some firms have decided to jazz things up a bit. The BIOS settings screen of our Asus board is quite pretty and tells you the time, the CPU temperature and how quickly the fan is running.

To get your PC to check for a boot CD or DVD before booting from the hard disk, we need to change the boot priority. In this case, that means using the arrow keys of the keyboard to enter the Boot Priority section, pressing Enter to select the hard disk, and using the left and right arrow keys to position it to the right of the CD/DVD drive. Press Enter when you've done this.

4

To leave this screen, press <ESC>. You'll now see three options: discard changes and exit, which takes your PC back to the settings it had before you went into the BIOS; save changes and reset, which applies your changes and reboots your PC; and Advanced Mode, which as you might expect takes you into the BIOS's advanced mode.

5

In this example, we'll go into Advanced Mode, which looks like an older, text-based BIOS screen and which provides extra options. Use the arrow keys to highlight your selection and Enter to select it. The BIOS will now let us see more information and, if we wish, edit more settings.

6

Navigating in Advanced Mode is simple: use the up and down arrow keys to move between the on-screen options and use the left and right arrow keys to move between the sections at the top (Main, AI Tweaker and so on). For example, to change the system time you use the down arrow to select it, press Enter, and type in the new values.

Use the right arrow to move to the AI Tweaker. We won't change any of the options here, but if you're an overclocker – someone who loves technology and wants to control every aspect of how their PC performs to get the maximum possible speed – you can adjust memory frequencies and CPU speeds here.

The next section, headed Advanced, enables you to configure onboard devices and connectors such as the SATA drives and USB ports. Once again, we'll leave the settings here as they are.

The Monitor section is fascinating. It tells you how warm the processor is, how warm the motherboard is, what speed the CPU fan is running at and it also allows you to change fan profiles for maximum cooling or minimum noise.

The Boot section enables you to specify what happens when you switch your PC on. For example, you can disable the full screen ASUS logo or change the boot priority, as we did in the initial BIOS screen.

The final part of the Advanced Mode interface enables you to use a flash utility to upgrade the motherboard's firmware, if that's something you need to do. Firmware is the software that's used by the motherboard to control everything and, from time to time, manufacturers issue downloadable firmware updates for their customers.

As with the simple mode, you can exit Advanced Mode by pressing <ESC>. You only get two options this time: Yes or No. If you select 'Yes' then the BIOS utility will apply the changes you've made; if you choose 'No' then it'll revert to the settings it had before you went into the BIOS utility.

PART  **Installing Windows**

Your brand-new PC is ready to run but without an operating system, such as Windows, it can't do anything useful. In this section, we'll discover what your options are and how to get Windows up and running on your PC.

When it comes to operating systems, you really have three choices: Windows 8, the latest version of Microsoft's operating system; Windows 7, the version of Windows before that, as the name suggests; and Linux, a free alternative operating system. Linux has lots of fans and won't cost you a penny but for maximum compatibility and ease of use we'd recommend Windows. For all its joys, Linux remains a little bit more complicated than Microsoft's offering. If you'd like to know more about Linux, however, have a look at **www.ubuntu.com**: it's one of the most-loved Linux versions and it's certainly one of the most user-friendly.

Bits and pieces

In this section, we're going to install the 64-bit version of Windows 8. Microsoft seems to have psychic knowledge of when we're working on a new *Build Your Own Computer* book, because every time we do there's a brand new version of Windows due for release a few days after our book goes to print. This edition is no exception and Windows 8 won't be released until shortly after this edition hits the shops. We've used the Consumer Preview of Windows 8, which is effectively the same thing as the version of Windows you'll find in the shops.

Why Windows 8? The first answer is that Windows 8 is a very good operating system and it'll be standard on new PCs from late 2012 onwards – so we want to show you the latest technology in this book. However, the new user interface, called Metro, has divided opinion: some people absolutely hate it. If you're one of them, Windows 7 is a perfectly good operating system, costs the same and installs the same way that Windows 8 does.

Why the 64-bit version? The reason we've gone for the 64-bit version is because that version takes full advantage of our freshly built PCs. In 32-bit mode, Windows can't access more than 4GB of RAM, and the only reason to consider 32-bit Windows these days is if you want to install older hardware such as TV tuners that might not have 64-bit device drivers (the software that tells Windows how to communicate with them). You don't need to make the final decision until you open the Windows box: it ships with discs for both 32-bit and 64-bit editions.

Which Windows?

Windows comes in several versions: there's Windows 8, Windows 8 Pro and Windows RT, not to mention multiple versions of Windows 7. In some cases, the choice is made for you. For example, Windows RT is only available pre-installed on devices such as tablet computers and can't be bought separately and Windows 7 Enterprise is only available to corporate users who buy in bulk. That still leaves us with a lot of different versions, however. Which one do you need?

- **Windows 8 and Windows 8 Pro**   Windows 8 is available in two flavours: Windows 8, which is aimed at home users, and Windows 8 Pro, which is aimed at business users and technology enthusiasts. For most people, the standard version is the one to get. If you want Windows Media Center, Microsoft's home entertainment software, you'll need to buy the Pro version.

With Windows 7 things are a little bit more complicated, and for home and small business users there are four versions to consider. They are:

- **Windows 7 Home Basic**   The Home Basic edition of Windows is slightly cheaper than the others, but it's missing some key features too. There's no Windows Media Center or DVD playback, you can't run older programs in Windows XP mode, and you can't take advantage of security features such as Bitlocker drive encryption. Although technically Home Basic is available in 64-bit and 32-bit flavours, you only get the 32-bit disc – and if you've got more than 8GB of memory, Home Basic won't look beyond the first eight.
- **Windows 7 Home Premium**   This one's the pick for us: this time you get Windows Media Center and DVD playback, support for multiple monitors and 16GB of RAM and easy HomeGroup networking. There are no business-class features such as drive encryption, though.
- **Windows 7 Professional**   This version of Windows is supposedly a no-nonsense version for business users, but it's actually Home Premium with some extra bells on: you even get Home Premium's free games, although they're disabled by default. Professional is essentially Home Premium with encrypted files and better support for networking but, surprisingly, not Bitlocker drive encryption.
- **Windows 7 Ultimate**   The Ultimate Edition delivers more Windows than you can shake a stick at: it's got everything its siblings have plus lots of features for power users, which are almost certainly going to be useless to you and to us.

Of all the versions of Windows 7, we think Home Premium is the smart choice: it offers all the features you need without adding lots of things you don't, and it's relatively cheap: while the Ultimate edition is around £130 at the time of writing, the Home Premium edition is around £80. You can shave another £10 off that by buying the OEM edition.

To OEM or not to OEM

OEM (Original Equipment Manufacturer) versions of Windows are designed specifically for system builders. That's you! They come in plain packaging rather than fancy retail boxes, they cost a little bit less than the packaged version and there are two things you need to know about them: they don't entitle you to any technical support at all and they're tied to one PC – so you can't take the OEM version you installed on one PC and put it on a newer PC in a year's time. Our advice: shop around, because you can sometimes get the full retail version for the same price as the OEM version.

It's worth mentioning that every copy of Windows includes a feature called Anytime Upgrade: if you decide that the version of Windows you've chosen isn't quite powerful enough for you, Anytime Upgrade enables you to unlock a more powerful edition of Windows. This, of course, costs money.

All genuine Windows discs are printed with intricate holograms. If yours doesn't have one, stop now: Windows has to be activated online and fake copies can't be activated. That means they stop working fully after 30 days.

Of all the various versions of Windows, we think the Home Premium edition offers the best value for money.

Installing Windows 8

Let's install Windows on our new PC. The version we're using here is the Consumer Preview, so the screens may differ very slightly from the released version but any differences will be slight. The Windows 7 installation routine is almost identical.

Turn on your PC and insert the Windows installation DVD immediately. When you see the message 'press any key to boot from CD/DVD', press any key on the keyboard. After a bit of churning you should see the first Windows installation screen.

Change the installation options from the US defaults to the UK options for language, time and currency format and keyboard layout. Press Next to continue.

3

Screens don't get much simpler than this: there's a great big Install Now button in the middle. It would be churlish not to click it.

4

Before you can continue, you'll need to provide a product key. This key is unique to each copy of Windows and you'll find it on a sticker on the back of the Windows box. Enter the key and then press the Next button.

5

Now, you'll be presented with the extremely long licensing agreement that nobody other than Microsoft's lawyers ever reads. We could be signing away our very souls for all we know but so far simply clicking 'I accept the license terms' and then pressing Next hasn't caused us any problems, so you might as well do it too.

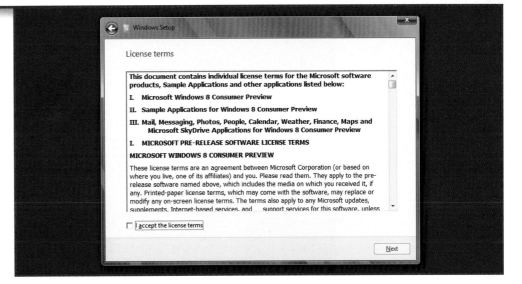

The Windows installer will now ask whether you want to perform an upgrade of an existing installation or whether you want to do a custom installation. We want the latter option as we're installing Windows on this PC for the very first time. If your disk is an OEM version, the custom option will be the only one available: the upgrade option will be greyed out.

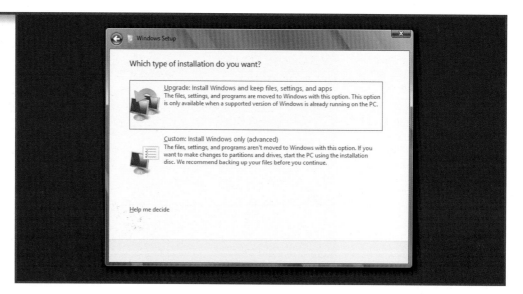

Windows will now ask you which disk drive you want to install it on. Unless you've installed more than one hard disk, you can simply click on Next here.

Time to put the kettle on: Windows will now install all of the necessary files on your PC, a process that can take a considerable amount of time. Your PC will restart a few times during this part of the installation process. That's perfectly normal and nothing to worry about.

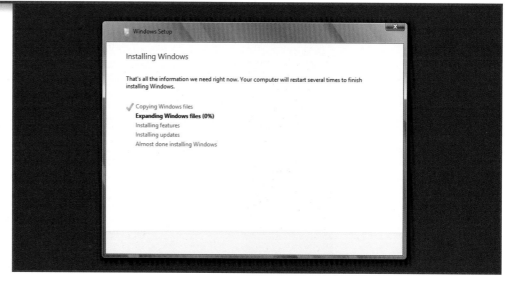

When all the files have been copied, Windows will ask you to give your PC a name. This shouldn't contain any spaces. Type the name in and press Next. This screen is from Windows 8; the Windows 7 one looks different but asks the same question.

To save time, Windows lets you use Express Settings for a quicker setup of your new copy of Windows. Click on Use Express Settings to continue.

Windows 8 uses your email address to sign you in to your PC. To get the best from it, you'll need a free Microsoft account. Enter your email address here and click Next. You won't be asked to do this if you're installing Windows 7, as it doesn't use a Microsoft account for any key features.

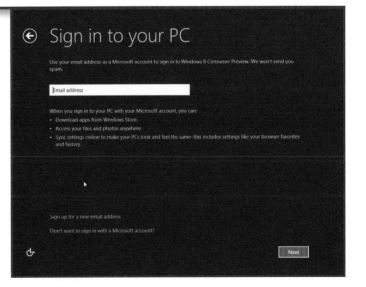

If you've already signed up for a Microsoft account (as we have), you'll be asked for your password. After you've provided that, Windows will ask for your mobile phone number so it can send you a login code if you accidentally lock yourself out of your PC. Enter your number but omit the first zero of the dialling code.

And here it is: Windows 8. It's very different from previous versions of Windows and we think it's much more fun than its predecessors.

Don't worry, the old Windows hasn't disappeared: if you click on the tile marked Desktop you'll see the familiar Windows Desktop. It's there to ensure any older software still works on Windows 8.

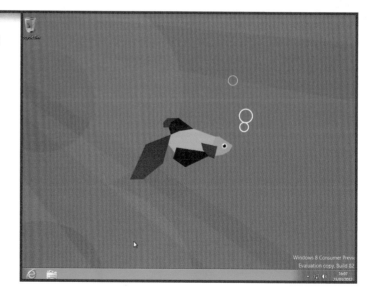

Driving you crazy

Once you've installed Windows, you'll need to install device drivers. Drivers are little software programs that enable Windows to communicate effectively with your hardware and, without them, things might not work properly. Your motherboard will have come with a CD or DVD of device drivers; additional hardware, such as wireless network cards or graphics cards, also come with driver discs. Once Windows is up and running, you should install the software from these discs as soon as you can for optimum performance and to eradicate any potential hardware hassles.

Getting online

If you want to use the internet you'll need an Ethernet cable to connect to your broadband router or a wireless internet adapter. The former plugs into the Ethernet socket on the back of your PC's motherboard and the latter fits into a spare USB port. Wireless is more convenient but Ethernet is faster — although for everyday browsing you don't need to worry too much about that.

Here's the result of all your hard work and the odd cut finger: a brand-new, home-made PC running Windows 8. This would be a good time to give yourself a pat on the back or to do a happy dance.

PART 5 Loose ends

You should now have a fully-functioning, home-built, better-than-off-the-shelf PC at your disposal. Congratulations – the hard work is done! If everything is behaving as it should, now is the time to consider further hardware installations to complete the picture.

In a mid-tower case such as this it's not always easy to clear away extraneous clutter. Just ensure that cables are kept well away from fans and check that airflow in and out of the case is not blocked. Here, the sound card's bracket cable is rather too close to the video card's heatsink.

There is one final, rather pressing matter to take care of, namely tidying your PC's interior. The trouble here is that there's no 'right' way to do it as such; it's really just a matter of bunching together surplus power cables and tucking them out of the way … somewhere. A free drive bay is fine. Keep dangling cables away from fans and other components, and ensure that, so far as possible, cables do not impede airflow through the case. Your computer case manufacturer may have included a few plastic cable ties, or else you can use your own. Avoid metal ties, even if coated in paper or plastic, as these could short-circuit the motherboard. Again, the benefits of a tall tower case with plenty of room are apparent, but even a mid- or mini-tower can be kept reasonably tidy.

A full-tower case is a cinch to keep tidy. This example is further helped by the use of round IDE/ATA cables instead of the usual flat ribbon cables and a side-mounted hard disk drive.

FINAL TOUCHES

Free software

You've spent every penny on your PC components but that doesn't mean you have to skimp on software: there's lots of great PC software that won't cost you a penny. You don't even have to go around the internet looking for it.

Software from Ninite

From time to time somebody creates a website that's so incredibly useful, you wonder why nobody thought of it before. Ninite (**www.ninite.com**) falls into that category: it's a one-stop shop for almost every free PC program you might need. It's fast and easy to use, too: all you need to do is to tick the items you want to download and then click on Get Installer. This creates a single download that installs everything you've selected. How clever is that?

These are the programs we'd recommend:

Chrome or Firefox Although every PC comes with Microsoft's Internet Explorer, many people prefer to use alternative browsers. At the time of writing, Google's Chrome is the fastest browser around while the Firefox browser is one of the most expandable.

Installing software doesn't get much easier than this: Ninite.com gives you a bunch of tick boxes and creates an installer for the programs you select.

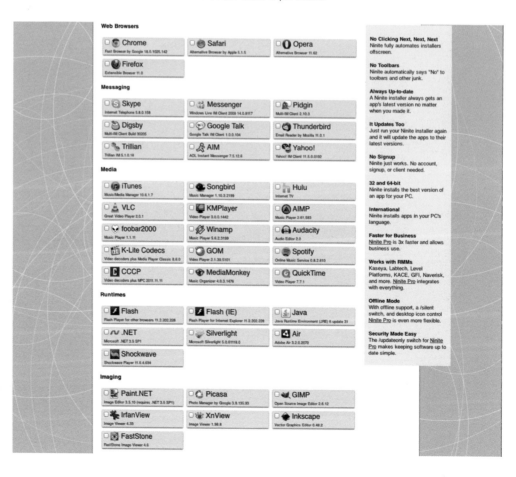

Skype   If you'd like to stay in touch with people without spending a fortune, the free Skype PC-to-PC voice and video chat service is a must-have. If you prefer text-based chat, Microsoft's Messenger and the multi-service Trillian are good choices too.

iTunes, VLC, Winamp, Audacity and Spotify   If you want to play media files, such as digital music or movies, then there are a number of useful programs here. iTunes is essential if you want to manage music on an iPod or iPhone (although it's hopeless if you don't), while Spotify provides free access to streaming music. Audacity is an excellent audio editing program for recording and messing around with sound, while VLC can play almost any kind of video file. If you plan to watch a lot of downloaded video, the K-Lite Codecs are worth having too: these give Windows the ability to handle pretty much any kind of video file you can imagine.

Flash and Silverlight   Many online applications are written in Adobe's Flash or Microsoft's Silverlight, so installing both on your new PC isn't a bad idea.

OpenOffice and Foxit Reader   OpenOffice is a free alternative to Microsoft Office. While it isn't quite as powerful as Microsoft's full suite, it isn't far off it. We take a detailed look at it over the page. Foxit Reader enables your PC to open PDF files (if you're running Windows 8, you don't need it; if you're running Windows 7, you do) and it isn't as big or as prone to annoying updates as the official Adobe Reader software.

Paint.net is free and surprisingly powerful. If you enjoy editing photos or creating digital art, it's well worth the download.

Other free options

Not every program you might want is available via Ninite. Here are a few more excellent programs you might like to download.

Windows Live Essentials   Available for free from **http://explore. live.com/windows-live-essentials**, Windows Live Essentials gives you the excellent Windows Live Mail email program, Photo Gallery for editing and organising your photos and Movie Maker for editing home videos.

Dropbox   If you want to share files across multiple devices, Dropbox (**www.dropbox.com)** is the way to do it: we used it in this book to share photographs between the photographer and writers. The program is free for 5GB of storage and works not just on PCs, but on smartphones, tablets and Apple computers too. It's enormously handy.

Paint.net   Paint.net (**www.getpaint.net**) started off as a lightweight alternative to the rather rubbish Paint program that comes with Windows. It's grown a bit since then and it's become a hugely impressive, fully featured image editor that's great for adjusting photographs or creating new drawings.

TECHIE CORNER

Free as a bird

Open Source is all about free software. However, while most of the best-known programs are indeed free, the movement's philosophy is free as in 'free speech' rather than 'free beer': there's nothing to stop firms making their own versions of open source programs and charging money for them, or offering programs on CD and then charging for the disc. However, most open source software, such as the excellent OpenOffice.org, are available for free download.

The open source movement is a reaction to traditional software firms, who release products but prohibit you from fiddling with them – so if you're a programmer who thinks Microsoft Word would be better if you did some tweaking, tough luck. The open source philosophy is best described as 'the more the merrier': the more people contributing their expertise to a program, the better the program will be. There are no secrets in open source, either. If you contribute to an open source program, you agree that others can look at what you've done and make changes to it. The result of all of this is a huge army of software developers producing some interesting products. In many cases, open source programs are better than anything from big name firms such as Microsoft or Apple.

Enough of the theory. What does this mean for you? Thanks to open source, you can get everything from your computer's operating system to a web browser, email program and even an entire office suite for free. You won't get technical support – in most cases if something goes wrong you're on your own – but when you see what you can get for nothing, we think you'll be impressed.

Can you really get decent office software for free?

The idea of a fully-featured Office suite for free sounds like we've been eating cheese before bedtime, but OpenOffice.org can do almost anything Microsoft Office can do. There's even a portable version you can stick on a USB thumb drive and carry around with you. The software is a free download from **www.openoffice.org** but we wouldn't recommend downloading it over a slow connection or a mobile one: the current Windows version is 144MB.

OpenOffice.org consists of five programs: Writer, which is quite like Microsoft Word; Calc, which resembles Excel; Impress, which is rather like PowerPoint; Draw, for images; and Base, for database work. The resemblance to Microsoft Office – albeit the Office of a few years ago rather than the current version – isn't an accident: the goal was always to create something Microsoft Office users would be happy with. The result is that you shouldn't have to hunt around too much to find familiar features.

The main problem for OpenOffice.org users is that people generally expect to receive Word's .doc files rather than OpenOffice files but you can make the software save in Word format by default: in Writer, go to Tools > Options > Load/save > General and then choose the Microsoft Word 97/2000/XP option. From now on, Writer will save in that format – although be aware that if you're using more complex features such as advanced formatting, not everything might work when it's saved as a Word document.

The big downside is that, as with all open source software, there's no formal technical support: if you get stuck or a feature doesn't work, it's up to you to Google for solutions. If you want the reassurance of having someone on the end of the phone you can talk to if things go wrong, then open source software might not be the right choice for you.

Security software

In previous issues we've urged you to install security software on your PC but, since Windows 7 was released, things have changed in that respect: every copy of Windows comes with its own security software, Windows Defender. If you're running Windows 7, it's worth also downloading Microsoft Security Essentials (**http://windows.microsoft.com/en-GB/windows/products/security-essentials**), which provides a better range of security scanning. You may not need to do that on Windows 8 as the built-in security has been beefed up again.

If you'd rather put your trust in third-party security software, there's plenty to choose from. We particularly like AVG Anti-Virus (**http://free.avg.com/gb-en/homepage**), AVAST Home Edition (www.avast.com) and ClamWin (**www.clamwin.com**), although Ninite.com has a few other options including the Spybot anti-spyware program.

Online offices

The programs we've looked at so far all have one thing in common: to use them, you need to install them on your PC. However, a new breed of programs works in a very different way; instead of installing them you simply access them through your Web browser. You can use word processing software, spreadsheet software, email software, calendar software ... if you can imagine it, there's probably a website that offers it. Even better, most such sites are free.

One of the best-known online suites is Google Docs & Spreadsheets (**http://docs.google.com**), which provides an excellent word processor, spreadsheet and, soon, a presentation

Google Docs & Spreadsheets provides basic word processing, spreadsheet and presentation features, and it all happens inside your Web browser.

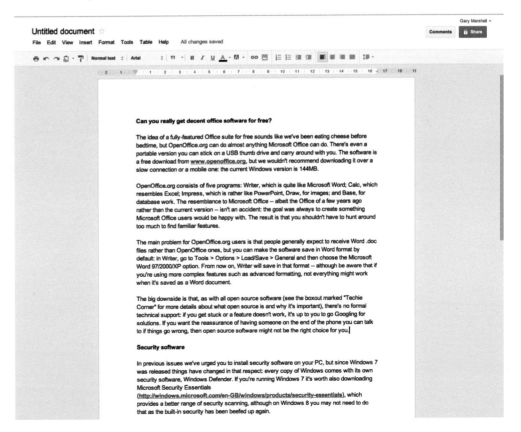

package inside your web browser. The programs are all free (although there are paid-for versions that provide you with extra storage) and work very well, and while they're not as powerful as OpenOffice.org they're not supposed to be. If all you need to do is bash out the odd letter or analyse a few figures, Google Docs & Spreadsheets will do the job quite happily.

Google isn't the only firm offering free, online software. Lots of sites offer online word processing and spreadsheet software, and some of the computer industry's biggest names are getting in on the act too. For example Adobe, whose Photoshop is the king of image-editing software, has announced its plans for a free, cut-down version of Photoshop Elements that you'll be able to access from any web browser.

Provided you have a broadband connection – dial-up modem connections just aren't fast enough – there are several key benefits to web-based software. In most cases, traditional software costs a great deal of money, but most online applications are free. They're also updated immediately, so if they need a security fix or a bug fix you don't need to download it. Instead, the next time you access the program you'll automatically use an updated version. Finally, many online programs enable you to store documents online, which means you can work from anywhere you can get internet access instead of having to carry your documents around with you on a USB flash drive or a CD-R.

Web wobbles

For all the benefits of using web-based programs, there are plenty of negatives too:

It's only as fast as your internet connection Online applications depend on computers that may be hundreds or even thousands of miles away, and if the connections between you and those computers are congested then the performance of the program will deteriorate dramatically.

No connection, no software In most cases, you can't access online software if you can't get online. Some services such as Google Docs enable you to work in offline mode when you're not connected to the internet, but if all your files are on Google's computer you won't be able to access them until you get back online.

It might not always be available We're big fans of online email systems such as Google Mail (**http://mail.google.com**), but we regularly encounter periods when the service isn't available – which means our email isn't available either. Other online services suffer from the same problems, so for example you might find that when you try to access the service to do something important it's 'temporarily unavailable' due to 'scheduled maintenance'.

There's no technical support With traditional software, there's usually a helpline you can call if you encounter trouble. With web-based software, there isn't.

If the site disappears, so does the software Google isn't likely to disappear any time soon, but what about the other online services? There are lots of me-too applications, for example, in the world of online word processors and spreadsheets there are

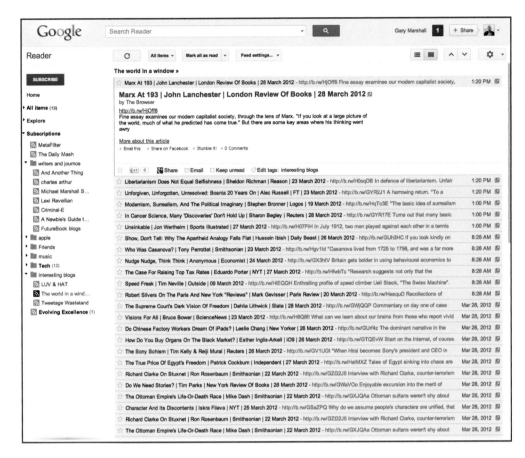

Although most web applications need an internet connection, a growing number can be used when you're not connected. Google Reader's newsreading program is one such package.

dozens of sites offering essentially the same kinds of software. Inevitably some of those sites won't last, and if you choose one of the ones that doesn't last the course then there's always the risk that it'll disappear overnight and take the software – and your documents – with it.

It might not be free forever Most online applications are free, especially the ones labelled 'beta' (more of that in a moment). However, there's no way to predict whether a particular program will stay free forever, or whether it'll cost money at a later date. If you come to depend on a particular program and the developers decide to charge for it, you'll either have to pay up or spend lots of time moving your data to an alternative program.

It's usually in beta If – like most online applications we've seen – a program is labelled as a 'beta' or a 'preview', that means it isn't finished. 'Beta' is computer industry shorthand for 'help us find the bugs', and it's generally accepted that beta software might do strange things, crash your computer or even destroy your data. That's fine if you want to experiment with cutting-edge technology, but if you use beta software (whether it's online or on your computer) for business-critical tasks then you're taking a very big risk.

Web-based services are improving quickly and in a few years, they could well be a better option than traditional programs. For basic Office tasks they're well worth considering, but for heavyweight jobs we'd stick with traditional software, whether that's a big-name package such as Microsoft Office or an open source alternative such as OpenOffice.org.

PART  Troubleshooting

Let's assume you've built your PC, turned it on for the first time ... and nothing happens. You can't get into BIOS, let alone install Windows. How and where do you begin to troubleshoot?

In fact, identifying a problem at this stage is very much easier than down the road when you've got a printer, scanner, webcam and goodness knows what other hardware attached; not to mention 57 software programs doing their utmost to interfere with one another, a real risk of viruses and perhaps a utility suite that does more harm than good. Your computer will never be so easy to diagnose and cure as it is right now.

Check the cables

The very first step is all too obvious but all too often overlooked: check that all external cables are securely connected in the correct places:

- [ ] The computer's PSU should be plugged into a mains wall socket (or power gangplank).

- [ ] So should the monitor.

- [ ] The mains electricity supply should be turned on at the wall.

- [ ] The monitor should be connected to the video card's VGA, DVI OR HDMI output.

- [ ] The keyboard should be connected to the computer's PS/2-style keyboard port (not to a USB port, unless USB support has already been enabled in BIOS, and not to the mouse port).

- [ ] The PSU should be set to the correct voltage and turned on.

Now turn on the monitor. A power indication LED on the monitor housing should illuminate and, hopefully, you'll see something on the screen. If not, re-read the monitor manual and double-check that you've correctly identified the on/off switch and are not busy fiddling with the brightness or contrast controls. It's not always obvious which switch is which. If the power light still does not come on, it sounds like the monitor itself may be at fault. Try changing the fuse in the cable. Ideally, test the monitor with another PC.

Internal inspection

Now turn on the PC itself. Press the large on/off switch on the front of the case, not the smaller reset switch. You should hear the whirring of internal fans and either a single beep or a sequence of beeps. But let's assume that all seems lifeless. Again, check/ change the fuse in the PSU power cable. If this doesn't help, unplug all cables, including the monitor, take off the case covers and lay the computer on its side. Now systematically check every internal connection. Again, here's a quick checklist to tick off:

- ☐ The PSU should be connected to the motherboard with a large 24-pin plug and also, if appropriate, with ATX 12V and ATX Auxiliary cables.
- ☐ The heatsink fan should be plugged into a power socket on the motherboard.
- ☐ The case fans should be likewise connected.
- ☐ All drives should be connected to the appropriate sockets on the motherboard with ribbon cables.
- ☐ All drives should be connected to the PSU with power cables.
- ☐ The video card should be securely sited in its AGP or PCI Express slot.
- ☐ All other expansion cards should be likewise in place.
- ☐ Look for loose screws inside the case, lest one should be causing a short-circuit.
- ☐ Check the front panel connections. If the case's on/off switch is disconnected from the motherboard, you won't be able to start the system.
- ☐ Are any cables snagging on fans?
- ☐ Are the retention clips on the memory DIMMs fully closed?
- ☐ Does anything on the motherboard look obviously broken or damaged?

Disconnect each cable in turn and look for bent pins on the plugs and sockets. These can usually be straightened with small, pointy pliers and a steady hand. Reconnect everything, including the monitor and power cable, and turn the computer on once more. Leave the covers off to aid observation. Does it now burst into life as if by magic? Rather gallingly, unplugging and replacing a cable is sometimes all it takes to fix an elusive but strictly temporary glitch.

PSU problems

Look for an LED on the motherboard (check the manual for its location). This should illuminate whenever the PSU is connected to the mains power and turned on, even when the computer itself is off. The LED confirms that the motherboard is receiving power; if it stays dark, the PSU itself may be at fault.

When you turn on the computer, do the fans remain static? Does the CD drive disc tray refuse to open? Is all depressingly dead? This would confirm the PSU as the problem. Use an alternative power cable, perhaps borrowed from the monitor, just to be sure. If still nothing happens, remove and replace the PSU.

NEVER TRY TO OPEN OR REPAIR A PSU. Nor should you try running it while it's disconnected from the motherboard, as a PSU can only operate with a load.

Next steps

Let's assume that there is evidence of power flowing to the motherboard: the LED comes on and the heatsink and case fans spin. The PSU must be okay but there's still nothing on the monitor screen. Did you hear a beep as the computer powered up? This is a good thing. A sequence of beeps is generally a sign – a welcome sign, in fact – of specific, identifiable trouble. See the Power On Self Test (POST) section on p.149.

Check the keyboard. If anything is resting on the keys, remove it. This alone can cause a computer to pause. As the computer powers up, three lights on the keyboard should illuminate within the first few seconds. If they fail to do so, it's just possible that a dud keyboard is responsible for halting the entire system. Disconnect it and reboot the computer without a keyboard attached. If you now see a keyboard error message on the monitor screen where all was blank before, it looks like you need a new one. Connect an alternative keyboard to the computer and reboot again to confirm the diagnosis.

Another clue: if the computer partially boots but then stalls, check the memory count during the POST procedure. If the RAM total differs from the memory you installed, it looks like you have a DIMM problem to deal with. Remove, clean and replace each module. If that gets you nowhere, try booting with a single module in place, and experiment with each in turn. Check the motherboard manual for details here; a single module must usually be installed in a specific DIMM slot (usually DIMM1). If you can start the computer successfully at some point, you should be able to identify and exclude faulty modules. This isn't much help if you only have one module, of course.

Back to basics

Failing all of the above, disconnect all power and ribbon cables from the drives and the motherboard. Unplug and remove the video card and any other expansion cards, disconnect the case fans and leave only a single memory module in place. In short, reduce the system to a bare bones configuration where the only remaining connections are between the PSU and the motherboard: ATX power, ATA Auxiliary and ATX 12V. Do not remove the heatsink or processor and leave all the front panel connections in place.

Now turn on the power once more. You should hear some diagnostic beeps from the BIOS. If so, see the following POST section and Appendix 3. If not, check the speaker connection.

If that doesn't resolve matters, turn off the computer, remove the power cable, and gradually, carefully, step-by-step, put it all back together again. Begin with the video card. Connect a monitor you know to be working and reboot the system. This will give you the added benefit of being able to read any onscreen error messages as you go along. If the screen stays blank, you know for sure that the video card is at fault. Replace it.

Reconnect a functioning keyboard next. Reboot and check that your computer gets past POST – i.e. that you can successfully enter the BIOS Setup routine. Now reconnect the floppy drive ribbon and power cables and reboot once more. Reinstall the hard disk drive next, followed by the CD and DVD drives. Every step of the way, reboot the computer and ensure that it doesn't hang or abort during POST. At some point, the computer may refuse to start – and right there you will have identified your problem. Alternatively, it may start normally all the way through

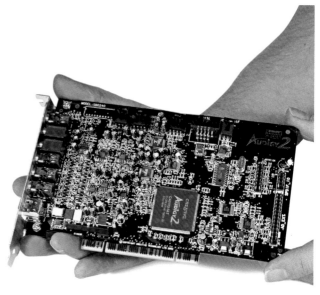

When handling expansion cards, be very careful not to touch either their onboard components or the lower gold connecting edge. With a card out of its slot, take the opportunity to clean its connecting edge with a lint-free cloth.

and you may never find out what the original stumbling block was. No matter: either way, you have successfully solved your hardware hassles.

Power On Self Test (POST)

The very first thing a computer does when it starts is give itself a quick once-over to check that it still has a processor, memory and motherboard. If this POST procedure finds a serious problem, or 'fatal error', it is likely to throw a wobbly and halt the computer in its tracks. That's the assumption we have been working on in this section.

However, it also gives you two useful diagnostic clues (actually three, but hexadecimal checkpoint codes are beyond the scope of this book).

First, assuming that the video card and monitor are both working, you should see some onscreen error messages. These may be self-explanatory or relatively obscure, depending on the problem and the BIOS manufacturer, but should offer at least some help. A memory error would indicate that one or more of your modules is either faulty or not properly installed; a 'hard disk not found' message would most likely point to a loose connection or perhaps a faulty cable.

Secondly, so long as the case speaker is connected, the motherboard will emit a series of POST-generated beeps. These can help you identify the specific component causing the problem.

We list some common beep code and error messages in Appendix 3.

POST is a low-key but essential routine that the computer runs through before launching Windows or any other operating system. Keep an eye out for error messages on the screen and an ear out for beep codes.

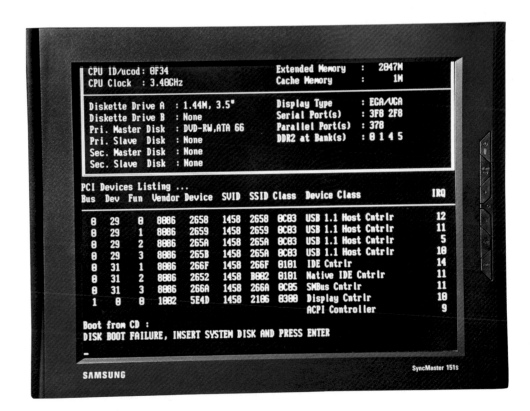

PART ⑥ Appendices

PART

Appendix 1
Silence is golden ... well, copper and aluminium

If there is one thing the average desktop computer is not, it is quiet. Gallingly, the more high-powered you make it, the noisier it becomes. It all boils down to the cooling systems inside the case, i.e. a bunch of low-tech fans. There are fans in the PSU, fans built into the case, a fan on the processor heatsink and yet another on the video card. Combined, they make a racket that's loud enough to be off-putting at best and to drown out music or game soundtracks at worst.

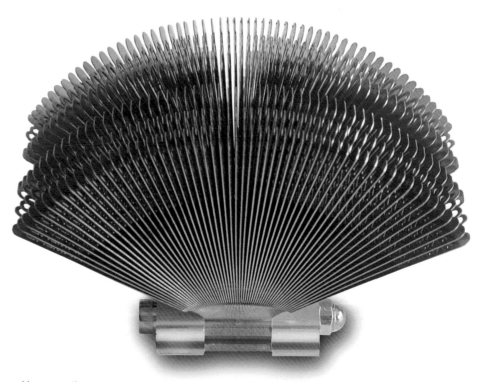

Freaky-looking it may be but this completely-silent Zalman 'Flower Cooler' can replace a boisterous CPU heatsink. All it needs is a really big, really quiet fan to supply it with fresh air.

However, there are some useful counter-measures available and here the DIY system builder can customise a computer to suit. For one, consider a passive heatsink for the processor, i.e. one without a powered fan. There are plenty of bizarre-looking but highly-effective heatsinks around that can keep the processor well within acceptable temperature limits (under 75° Celsius for a typical processor).

Even chipset fans tend to be irritatingly intrusive, so you might care to remove the northbridge heatsink and replace it with a silent fan-less alternative.

Most recent video cards also use fan-assisted heatsinks to cool the GPU. Here again it is often possible to replace the original with a silent version. Be careful, though: some of the latest video chips run so hot that a passive heatsink alone is not sufficient unless there is also a fan nearby to supply cool air.

There's little to do about a noisy PSU other than replace it with a quiet one – or, of course, to buy a quiet PSU in the first place. Check the specs and look for an acoustic noise level of about 30dB when the unit is running at 75% capacity.

Going further, you can even encase the hard disk drive in an acoustic enclosure and clad the interior of the case with sound-muffling panels.

Cooling caveats

Just a couple:

1. In smaller cases, the PSU is often located directly above the processor socket. This generally rules out a passive heatsink because there simply isn't the necessary clearance over the processor. And even if you can squeeze one into the available space, don't forget that …

2. Even an elaborate super-effective passive heatsink needs some independent cooling. This is generally provided by a large, variable-speed ultra-quiet fan positioned directly above the heatsink and held in place with an angled bracket attached to the case. Again, this is not possible in most mid-tower cases.

In short, don't shell out for an inventive cooling solution unless you're sure your case can accommodate it. If you have an unobstructed view of the processor socket when the motherboard and PSU are both in place inside the case, you should be OK.

Consult Quiet PC for specialist advice and products, including the Zalman range of silent heatsinks (see Appendix 4).

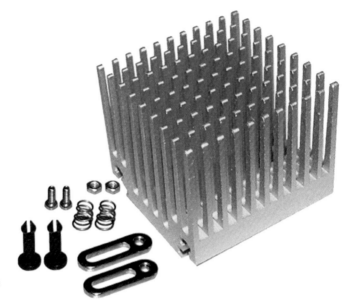

If your chipset has a fan, consider replacing it with an efficient passive heatsink. So long as there is reasonable airflow inside the case, this will keep it cool and quiet.

If even the clicking of the hard disk drive drives you to distraction, encase your case in mufflers.

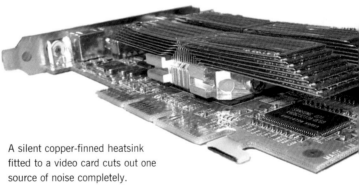

A silent copper-finned heatsink fitted to a video card cuts out one source of noise completely.

APPENDICES

PART 6 Appendix 2
That's entertainment: making a media centre PC

If your PC lives in a spare bedroom you might not be using its full potential: these days even the humblest PC is an entertainment powerhouse. So why not put it in the living room?

The computer you've built with the help of this book isn't just a powerful business and gaming machine. With the right software, a couple of components and a few simple tweaks it can be an all-singing, all-dancing multimedia marvel, so it's a shame to keep it tucked away in a spare bedroom or the study.

If like us you plumped for the Home Premium edition of Windows, all the software you need is already sitting on your PC – and if you also installed a TV tuner card, all the hardware you need is there too.

Here's what your PC can do:

- It's a fully featured DVD player and you can connect your sound card to your stereo for stunning soundtracks.
- It's a digital jukebox that can store all your music and even your music videos, playing them through your TV or your hi-fi.
- It's a CD maker that you can use to burn your own compilation CDs.
- It's a movie marvel that can import and edit movies and then publish them to DVD.
- It's a showcase for your digital photos with special effects, videos and slideshows.
- It's a radio and an internet radio receiver.
- It's a digital video recorder that can record two channels at once – and it works with Freeview channels too.

This is an off-the-shelf Media Center PC but you can just as easily build your own. Note the digital TV tuner card, which is all you need to receive Freeview channels.

Windows 7 Home Premium, Windows 7 Ultimate and Windows 8 Pro include Media Center, which is designed to turn your PC into a multimedia marvel.

- It's a door to a world of movie downloads, broadband TV and digital music.
- It's a home entertainment hub that can stream music to an Xbox 360.
- It's a games machine with graphics that consoles can only dream of.

Not bad for a humble PC, eh? However, to get the best from your PC's media features it's worth considering a few issues.

Think before you build it
A tower PC like the one we built in Part 3 might not be ideal for your living room, particularly if you're short of space or would prefer not to have a massive box in the corner. Noise is an issue too: a PC case with lots of fans can be very noisy and you don't want the quiet bits of a film spoiled by a PC that sounds like a jumbo jet. In many cases, you'd be better off with a small form factor PC like the one we built in Part 4, which is small enough to fit under your TV and quiet enough to do the job without spoiling your enjoyment.

Another option worth considering is a media centre case. Such cases are designed to blend in with the other equipment underneath your TV and, in addition to looking good, they're also designed to be quiet. In most cases you'll find that media centre cases follow the MicroATX standard, so there should be a wide selection of motherboards to choose from. Most of the major case manufacturers offer media centre cases and prices range from around £40 for a cheap and cheerful model to over £100 for something that looks like a really expensive hi-fi component.

Choose the right version of Windows
No matter which edition of Windows you choose, you'll get Windows Media Player. This can copy CDs and turn them into digital music files, play DVDs (and Blu-Ray discs if you've got a Blu-Ray compatible drive like the ones we used in our two PC projects) and manage your music collection. You'll find that any version of Windows is compatible with video-on-demand services, such as the BBC's iPlayer or Channel 4's 4oD, as well as with download shops such as Apple's iTunes.

If you're really serious about your media PC, you might also want to consider Windows 7 Home Premium, Windows 7 Ultimate or Windows 8 Pro, as these give you Windows Media Center. Where Windows is designed to be used from a distance of a few inches, Media Center is designed to be used from the sofa on a big-screen TV. It doesn't just handle movies: if you've installed a TV tuner, it can watch and record live TV and it also supports FM radio (again, if your hardware supports it) and viewing your stored photos.

Get a TV tuner, if you want one

Until recently using your PC as a personal video recorder was one of the most cost-effective ways to record TV digitally, but the rise of services from the likes of Sky and Virgin, as well as the growing popularity of video-on-demand services, such as iPlayer, 4oD and Netflix, means that a TV tuner isn't as essential as it used to be: if you've got a reasonably fast broadband connection then you can get most TV without bothering with aerial or satellite dish connections.

That doesn't mean that a tuner is a bad idea, though, and if you fancy the convenience of a Sky+HD box or Virgin Media Tivo without the monthly cost then you can certainly build something as good as, and possibly much better than, any commercial offering. The trick is to find the right tuner, and to make sure it works with your version of Windows: not all tuners are available with the most up-to-date drivers and not all of them have 64-bit drivers for 64-bit versions of Windows. Always check Microsoft's Windows compatibility pages at **www.microsoft.com/windows/compatibility** before spending any money.

TV tuners come in two forms: as expansion cards that you install in much the same way as graphics cards and as USB sticks that simply pop into a spare USB port. The latter option is more portable – if you've got a laptop, you can take the TV tuner with you when you travel – but remember that it still needs to be connected to an aerial. Once it is, you can connect to Freeview TV broadcasts. If you plump for a satellite-compatible model, you can receive Freesat channels if you already have a satellite dish.

If you're investing in a TV tuner card or USB device, make sure it's digital: the UK's digital switchover is nearly complete and the few remaining analogue TV transmitters should have been switched off by the time you read this.

Make the right connections

If you're using your PC as a living room media centre you'll need to make a few connections, and you might need to invest in a few cables too. You'll need to connect your sound card outputs to your stereo (or just use a dedicated set of good quality PC speakers); you'll need to connect your TV tuner card to your TV aerial; and you'll need to connect your PC's video card to your TV. With modern flat screen TVs that's usually straightforward, as most of them have either VGA connectors or DVI connectors that accept standard VGA or DVI cables. With older TVs you'll need to use your video card's TV-out connector.

Cut the cables

Cables aren't always a good thing, especially if they're trailing across your carpet. In addition to a remote control, a wireless keyboard and mouse is a good investment. Early models had shockingly bad battery life but these days, wireless peripherals run for weeks and weeks on a single set of batteries – and you can hide them when you're not using them. A wireless keyboard comes in particularly handy if you want to play games or surf the internet on your big-screen TV but don't fancy sitting with your nose pressed up against it.

Another option: the home hub

Sticking your PC under the TV isn't the only way to take advantage of its entertainment possibilities. You could make it the hub of a home entertainment network too. Don't worry, it's much simpler and cheaper than it sounds!

The idea behind a home hub is that your PC stores all your stuff, but other devices can access it. For example, if you've already got an Xbox 360 in the living room you can get it to share data with your PC, which means your Xbox can access your PC's music, your movies and your digital photo collection. Once again Windows Vista includes the necessary software, so both Windows Media Player and the Windows Vista Media Center can stream software to other PCs or to your Xbox 360.

For that software to work, though, you'll need a network connection between your Xbox and your PC. A wireless network is the obvious answer, but it isn't always perfect. If your house is full of brick walls and other solid structures or your Xbox is located quite far away from your wireless networking adapter, you might find that the wireless signal is weak and that the connection speed suffers as a result. That's not a problem for streaming photos, but a patchy signal can seriously affect the quality of streaming music and render video unwatchable.

If you have a less than perfect wireless signal, your network may not be fast enough for really high quality video streaming – but that doesn't mean you need to start drilling holes and running Ethernet network cables everywhere. Thanks to powerline networking you can get Ethernet speeds without Ethernet cables.

Powerline networking is enormously clever. Instead of using wireless signals, it uses your house's electricity circuit to deliver network data. All you need is two adapters: one for your PC or router and one for your Xbox or second PC. Connect each adapter to the appropriate equipment (the cables you need come in the box) and then it's just a matter of plugging each one into a spare wall socket and switching it on. After around 20 seconds the adapters will connect to one another and you'll have faster-than-wireless networking speeds without any drilling or cable clutter.

Early powerline equipment was fairly slow, but current models are as fast as normal Ethernet networks. Look for devices offering speeds of 85Mbps or higher and, as ever, take such speeds with a pinch of salt: in the real world, you'll probably get speeds of around one-quarter to one-half of the quoted maximums. That's still much faster than wireless, though, and it's probably much faster than your broadband connection too. Expect to pay around £100 for a high-speed kit that includes everything you need to connect two devices.

If that's whetted your appetite for entertainment and you'd like to know even more, including alternative hardware and software options, check out our *PC Home Entertainment Manual*.

If you've got an Xbox 360, you can stream music, movies and photos to it from your Windows PC over a wired or wireless network.

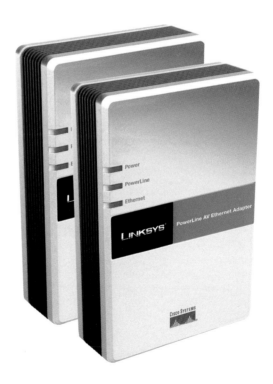

Powerline networking equipment transmits data via your house's existing electrical wiring. It's ideal for houses where wireless networks don't deliver.

Appendix 3
Beep and error codes

As we discussed earlier, the motherboard – or more precisely, the BIOS chip on the motherboard – emits a sequence of beeps whenever it identifies a problem that is serious enough to prevent the computer from starting normally. If the BIOS does manage to get the computer up and running, it can also generate onscreen error messages that help you identify trouble spots. Here we reprint the codes used by AMI and Award, makers of two commonly used BIOS programs.

Phoenix, another major player, uses a rather more complicated scheme that is beyond our scope here.

AMI BIOS beep codes

Number of Beeps	Problem	Action
1	Memory refresh timer error.	Remove each memory module, clean the connecting edge that plugs into the motherboard socket, and replace. If that doesn't work, try restarting with a single memory module and see if you can identify the culprit by a process of elimination. If you still get the error code, replace with known good modules.
2	Parity error.	As with 1 beep above.
3	Main memory read/write test error.	As with 1 beep above.
4	Motherboard timer not operational.	Either the motherboard is faulty or one of the expansion cards has a problem. Remove all cards except the video card and restart. If the motherboard still issues this beep code, it has a serious, probably fatal problem. If the beeps stop, replace the cards one at a time and restart each time. This should identify the guilty party.
5	Processor error.	As with 4 beeps above.
6	Keyboard controller BAT test error.	As with 4 beeps above.
7	General exception error.	As with 4 beeps above.
8	Display memory error.	The video card is missing, faulty or incorrectly installed. Remove, clean the connecting contacts and replace. If that doesn't work, try using a different video card. If you are using integrated video instead of a video card, the motherboard may be faulty.
9	ROM checksum error.	As with 4 beeps above.
10	CMOS shutdown register read/write error.	As with 4 beeps above.
11	Cache memory bad.	As with 4 beeps above.

AMIBIOS8 Checkpoint and Beep Code List version 1.2. Copyright of American Megatrends, Inc. Reprinted with permission. All rights reserved.

AMI BIOS error codes
Here are some examples of onscreen error messages:

Error	Action
Gate20 Error	The BIOS is unable to properly control the motherboard's Gate A20 function, which controls access of memory over 1MB. This may indicate a problem with the motherboard.
Multi-Bit ECC Error	This message will only occur on systems using ECC-enabled memory modules. ECC memory has the ability to correct single-bit errors that may occur from faulty memory modules. A multiple bit corruption of memory has occurred, and the ECC memory algorithm cannot correct it. This may indicate a defective memory module.
Parity Error	Fatal Memory Parity Error. System halts after displaying this message.
Boot Failure	This is a generic message indicating the BIOS could not boot from a particular device. This message is usually followed by other information concerning the device.
Invalid Boot Diskette	A diskette was found in the drive, but it is not configured as a bootable diskette.
Drive Not Ready	The BIOS was unable to access the drive because it indicated it was not ready for data transfer. This is often reported by drives when no media is present.
A: Drive Error	The BIOS attempted to configure the A: drive during POST, but was unable to properly configure the device. This may be because of a bad cable or faulty diskette drive.
Insert BOOT diskette in A:	The BIOS attempted to boot from the A: drive, but could not find a proper boot diskette.
Reboot and Select proper Boot device or Insert Boot Media in selected Boot device	BIOS could not find a bootable device in the system and/or removable media drive does not contain media.
NO ROM BASIC	This message occurs on some systems when no bootable device can be detected.
Primary Master Hard Disk Error	The IDE/ATAPI device configured as Primary Master could not be properly initialized by the BIOS. This message is typically displayed when the BIOS is trying to detect and configure IDE/ATAPI devices in POST.
Primary Slave Hard Disk Error	The IDE/ATAPI device configured as Primary Slave could not be properly initialized by the BIOS. This message is typically displayed when the BIOS is trying to detect and configure IDE/ATAPI devices in POST.
Secondary Master Hard Disk Error	The IDE/ATAPI device configured as Secondary Master could not be properly initialized by the BIOS. This message is typically displayed when the BIOS is trying to detect and configure IDE/ATAPI devices in POST.
Secondary Slave Hard Disk Error	The IDE/ATAPI device configured as Secondary Slave could not be properly initialized by the BIOS. This message is typically displayed when the BIOS is trying to detect and configure IDE/ATAPI devices in POST.

AMI BIOS error codes continued:

Error	Action
Primary Master Drive – ATAPI Incompatible	The IDE/ATAPI device configured as Primary Master failed an ATAPI compatibility test. This message is typically displayed when the BIOS is trying to detect and configure IDE/ATAPI devices in POST.
Primary Slave Drive – ATAPI Incompatible	The IDE/ATAPI device configured as Primary Slave failed an ATAPI compatibility test. This message is typically displayed when the BIOS is trying to detect and configure IDE/ATAPI devices in POST.
Secondary Master Drive – ATAPI Incompatible	The IDE/ATAPI device configured as Secondary Master failed an ATAPI compatibility test. This message is typically displayed when the BIOS is trying to detect and configure IDE/ATAPI devices in POST.
Secondary Slave Drive – ATAPI Incompatible	The IDE/ATAPI device configured as Secondary Slave failed an ATAPI compatibility test. This message is typically displayed when the BIOS is trying to detect and configure IDE/ATAPI devices in POST.
S.M.A.R.T. Capable but Command Failed	The BIOS tried to send a S.M.A.R.T. message to a hard disk, but the command transaction failed. This message can be reported by an ATAPI device using the S.M.A.R.T. error reporting standard. S.M.A.R.T. failure messages may indicate the need to replace the hard disk.
S.M.A.R.T. Command Failed	The BIOS tried to send a S.M.A.R.T. message to a hard disk, but the command transaction failed. This message can be reported by an ATAPI device using the S.M.A.R.T. error reporting standard. S.M.A.R.T. failure messages may indicate the need to replace the hard disk.
S.M.A.R.T. Status BAD, Backup and Replace	A S.M.A.R.T. capable hard disk sends this message when it detects an imminent failure. This message can be reported by an ATAPI device using the S.M.A.R.T. error reporting standard. S.M.A.R.T. failure messages may indicate the need to replace the hard disk.
S.M.A.R.T. Capable and Status BAD	A S.M.A.R.T. capable hard disk sends this message when it detects an imminent failure. This message can be reported by an ATAPI device using the S.M.A.R.T. error reporting standard. S.M.A.R.T. failure messages may indicate the need to replace the hard disk.
BootSector Write!!	The BIOS has detected software attempting to write to a drive's boot sector. This is flagged as possible virus activity. This message will only be displayed if Virus Detection is enabled in AMIBIOS Setup.
VIRUS: Continue (Y/N)?	If the BIOS detects possible virus activity, it will prompt the user. This message will only be displayed if Virus Detection is enabled in AMIBIOS Setup.
DMA-2 Error	Error initializing secondary DMA controller. This is a fatal error, often indicating a problem with system hardware.
DMA Controller Error	POST error while trying to initialize the DMA controller. This is a fatal error, often indicating a problem with system hardware.

AMI BIOS error codes continued:

Error	Action
CMOS Date/Time Not Set	The CMOS Date and/or Time are invalid. This error can be resolved by readjusting the system time in AMIBIOS Setup.
CMOS Battery Low	CMOS Battery is low. This message usually indicates that the CMOS battery needs to be replaced. It could also appear when the user intentionally discharges the CMOS battery.
CMOS Settings Wrong	CMOS settings are invalid. This error can be resolved by using AMIBIOS Setup.
CMOS Checksum Bad	CMOS contents failed the Checksum check. Indicates that the CMOS data has been changed by a program other than the BIOS or that the CMOS is not retaining its data due to malfunction. This error can typically be resolved by using AMIBIOS Setup.
Keyboard Error	Keyboard is not present or the hardware is not responding when the keyboard controller is initialized.
Keyboard/Interface Error	Keyboard Controller failure. This may indicate a problem with system hardware.
System Halted	The system has been halted. A reset or power cycle is required to reboot the machine. This message appears after a fatal error has been detected.

Award BIOS beep codes

Number of Beeps	Problem	Action
1 long beep followed by 2 short beeps	Video card problem	Remove the card, clean the connecting edge that plugs into the motherboard socket, and replace. If that doesn't work, try an alternative video card to establish whether the problem lies with the card or the AGP slot. If you are using integrated video instead of a video card, the motherboard may be faulty.
Any other beeps	Memory problem	Remove each memory module, clean the connecting edge that plugs into the motherboard socket, and replace. If that doesn't work, try restarting with a single memory module and see if you can identify the culprit by a process of elimination. If you still get the error code, replace with known good modules.

Award BIOS error codes
Here are the standard Award onscreen error messages:

Error	Action
BIOS ROM checksum error – System halted	The checksum of the BIOS code in the BIOS chip is incorrect, indicating the BIOS code may have become corrupt. Contact your system dealer to replace the BIOS.
CMOS battery failed	The CMOS battery is no longer functional. Contact your system dealer for a replacement battery.
CMOS checksum error – Defaults loaded	Checksum of CMOS is incorrect, so the system loads the default equipment configuration. A checksum error may indicate that CMOS has become corrupt. This error may have been caused by a weak battery. Check the battery and replace if necessary.
CPU at nnnn	Displays the running speed of the CPU.
Display switch is set incorrectly	The display switch on the motherboard can be set to either monochrome or colour. This message indicates the switch is set to a different setting from that indicated in Setup. Determine which setting is correct, and then either turn off the system and change the jumper, or enter Setup and change the VIDEO selection.
Press ESC to skip memory test	The user may press Esc to skip the full memory test.
Floppy disk(s) fail	Cannot find or initialize the floppy drive controller or the drive. Make sure the controller is installed correctly. If no floppy drives are installed, be sure the Diskette Drive selection in Setup is set to NONE or AUTO.
HARD DISK initializing. Please wait a moment.	Some hard drives require extra time to initialize.
HARD DISK INSTALL FAILURE	Cannot find or initialize the hard drive controller or the drive. Make sure the controller is installed correctly. If no hard drives are installed, be sure the Hard Drive selection in Setup is set to NONE.
Hard disk(s) diagnosis fail	The system may run specific disk diagnostic routines. This message appears if one or more hard disks return an error when the diagnostics run.
Keyboard error or no keyboard present	Cannot initialize the keyboard. Make sure the keyboard is attached correctly and no keys are pressed during POST. To purposely configure the system without a keyboard, set the error halt condition in Setup to HALT ON ALL, BUT KEYBOARD. The BIOS then ignores the missing keyboard during POST.
Keyboard is locked out – Unlock the key	This message usually indicates that one or more keys have been pressed during the keyboard tests. Be sure no objects are resting on the keyboard.
Memory Test	This message displays during a full memory test, counting down the memory areas being tested.
Memory test fail	If POST detects an error during memory testing, additional information appears giving specifics about the type and location of the memory error.
Override enabled – Defaults loaded	If the system cannot boot using the current CMOS configuration, the BIOS can override the current configuration with a set of BIOS defaults designed for the most stable, minimal-performance system operations.
Press TAB to show POST screen	System OEMs may replace the Phoenix Technologies' AwardBIOS POST display with their own proprietary display. Including this message in the OEM display permits the operator to switch between the OEM display and the default POST display.
Primary master hard disk fail	POST detects an error in the primary master IDE hard drive.
Primary slave hard disk fail	POST detects an error in the primary slave IDE hard drive.
Secondary master hard disk fail	POST detects an error in the secondary master IDE hard drive.
Secondary slave hard disk fail	POST detects an error in the secondary slave IDE hard drive.

PART 6 Appendix 4 Further resources

Here are some links you might find useful when it comes to learning more about components, finding the best deals, getting software and understanding your consumer rights. Please note that if we've listed a retailer that isn't necessarily a recommendation: it always pays to shop around.

Component suppliers

Amazon UK	www.amazon.co.uk
CCL	www.cclonline.com
Crucial (memory)	www.crucial.com/uk
Dabs	www.dabs.com
eBuyer	www.ebuyer.com
Kingston (memory)	www.kingston.com/en
Morgan Computers	www.morgancomputers.co.uk
MyMemory	www.mymemory.co.uk
Overclockers	www.overclockers.co.uk
Quiet PC	www.quietpc.com

Don't forget the High Street, either: you'll often find decent deals in the big-name retailers via Managers' Specials, end-of-line deals and so on. Independent computer shops can be a great source of hardware, advice and support too.

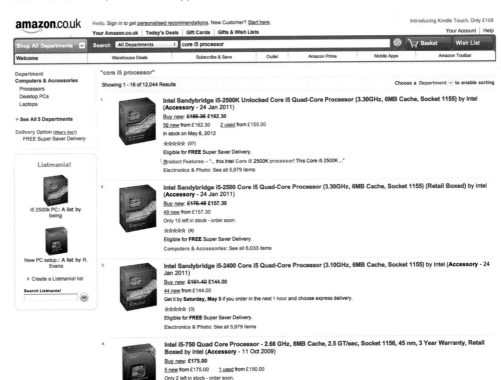

Computer fairs

British Computer Fairs	www.britishcomputerfairs.com
Northern Computer Markets	www.computermarkets.co.uk

Price checkers and cashback sites

Google Product Search	www.google.co.uk/shopping
Kelkoo	www.kelkoo.co.uk
Quidco (cashback)	www.quidco.com

Consumer rights

DirectGov	www.direct.gov.uk/en/Governmentcitizensandrights/Consumerrights/index.htm
Office of Fair Trading	www.oft.gov.uk
Trading Standards	www.tradingstandards.gov.uk

Processors, motherboards and chipset information

AMD	www.amd.com
Asus	http://uk.asus.com/motherboards
Intel	www.intel.com
NVIDIA	www.nvidia.co.uk

Hardware review sites

Anandtech	www.anandtech.com
Ars Technica	http://arstechnica.com
Extreme Tech	www.extremetech.com
Hardware Secrets	www.hardwaresecrets.com
Techradar	www.techradar.com/news/computing-components
Tom's Hardware Guide	www.tomshardware.co.uk

Software

AVAST anti-virus	www.avast.com
AVG anti-virus	http://free.avg.com/gb-en/homepage
ClamWin anti-virus	www.clamwin.com
DropBox	www.dropbox.com
Google Docs	http://docs.google.com
Ninite	www.ninite.com
OpenOffice.org	www.openoffice.org
Paint.net	www.getpaint.net
Windows Live Essentials	http://get.live.com

Appendix 5
Abbreviations & acronyms

A handy list of some shorthand terms used throughout
this manual or that you might otherwise encounter.

2D/3D	Two-dimensional/three-dimensional		HDCP	High-bandwidth Digital Content Protection
2x/4x, etc.	Double-speed/quadruple-speed, etc.		HDD	Hard Disk Drive
A3D	Aureal 3D		HDMI	High Definition Media Interface
AC '97	Audio Codec '97		HT	Hyper-Threading
AGP	Accelerate Graphics Port		I/O	Input/Output
AMR	Audio Modem Riser		ICH	Integrated Controller Hub
ASIO	Audio Stream In/Out		IDE	Integrated Drive Electronics
ATA	Advanced Technology Attachment		IEC	International Electrotechnical Commission
ATAPI	Advanced Technology Attachment Packet Interface		IEEE	Institute of Electrical and Electronic Engineers
ATX	Advanced Technology Extended		ISA	Industry Standard Architecture
BD	Blu-Ray disc		KB	Kilobyte
BD-R	Recordable Blu-Ray disc		KHz	Kilohertz
BD-RE	Rewritable Blu-Ray disc		LAN	Local Area Network
BD-ROM	Read-only Blu-Ray disc		LED	Light-Emitting Diode
BIOS	Basic In/Out System		MB	Megabyte
CD	Compact Disc		Mbps	Megabits per second
CD-DA	Compact Disc – Digital Audio		MHz	Megahertz
CD-R	Compact Disc – Recordable		MIDI	Musical Instrument Digital Interface
CD-ROM	Compact Disc – Read-Only Memory		MP3	Motion Picture Experts Group Audio Layer Three
CD-RW	Compact Disc – Rewriteable		MPEG	Motion Picture Experts Group
CMOS	Complementary Metal-Oxide Semiconductor		NIC	Network Interface Card
CNR	Communications and Networking Riser		NTFS	New Technology File System
CPU	Central Processing Unit		PC	Personal Computer
DAE	Digital Audio Extraction		PCI	Peripheral Component Interconnect
dB	Decibel		PnP	Plug-and-Play
DDR-RAM	Double Data Rate – Random-Access Memory		POST	Power On Self Test
DIMM	Dual Inline Memory Module		PS/2	Personal System/2
DMA	Direct Memory Access		PSU	Power Supply Unit
DSL	Digital Subscriber Line		RAID	Redundant Array of Independent Disks
DTS	Digital Theatre Systems		RAM	Random-Access Memory
DVD	Digital Versatile Disc		S.M.A.R.T.	Self-Monitoring Analysis and Reporting Technology
DVD-RAM	Digital Versatile Disc – Random-Access Memory		SATA	Serial Advanced Technology Attachment
DVD-ROM	Digital Versatile Disc – Read-Only Memory		SCSI	Small Computer Systems Interface
DVD-R/RW	Digital Versatile Disc – Recordable/Rewriteable		SD-RAM	Synchronous Dynamic – Random-Access Memory
DVD+R/RW	Digital Versatile Disc – Recordable/Rewriteable		SPDIF	Sony/Philips Digital Interface
DVI	Digital Visual Interface		SSD	Solid State Drive
EAX	Environmental Audio Extensions		TB	Terabyte
FAQ	Frequently Asked Questions		TFT	Thin Film Transistor
FAT	File Allocation Table		UPS	Uninterruptible Power Supply
FSB	Front Side Bus		USB	Universal Serial Port
GB	Gigabyte		VGA	Video Graphics Array
GHz	Gigahertz		Wi-Fi	Wireless Fidelity
GPU	Graphics Processing Unit		ZIF	Zero Insertion Force

Index

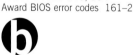

Authors	**Kyle MacRae and Gary Marshall**
Copy Editor	**Shena Deuchars**
Photography	**Iain McLean**
Page build	**James Robertson**
Index	**Shena Deuchars**
Project Manager	**Louise McIntyre**